THE
LAST PATROL

Policemen killed on duty
while serving in the
Thames Valley

Len Woodley

First published August 2001
by
The Book Castle
12 Church Street
Dunstable
Bedfordshire LU5 4RU

ISBN 1 90374 7 02 3
Typeset and Designed by Priory Graphics
Flitwick, Bedfordshire
Printed by Creative Print and Design Group
Harmondsworth, Middlesex

ABOUT THE AUTHOR

Buckinghamshire born, Leonard Woodley joined the local Police in 1956 straight from school and served at various stations throughout the county, in both uniform and in the Criminal Investigation Department. After retiring from the Police, he worked for the High Sheriff of the county and then for a number of years as a Patrol Officer for British Waterways. Finally he was a temporary Coroner's Officer for Milton Keynes before retiring completely. Now living within the boundaries of the new City with his wife, Leonard is still researching old murders.

CONTENTS

Page

SOURCES

NEWSPAPERS:

Oxford Herald, Oxford Journal, Oxford Times, Newbury Weekly News, Banbury Guardian, Oxford Mail, Rugby Advertiser, Kensington Post, Maidenhead Advertiser, Reading Evening Post, Reading Chronicle, Reading Mercury, Daily Telegraph, Daily Mirror, The Times, Illustrated Police News, Berkshire Chronicle, Daily Chronicle, Daily News, Wiltshire Gazette & Herald.

BOOKS:

Dobson, Bob; 'Policing in Lancashire, 1839-1989' (1989)
Gribble, Leonard; 'They Shot to Slay' (1986).
Indge, W; 'One Hundred Years - Berkshire Constabulary' (1956)
Josephs, Jeremy; 'Hungerford - One Man's Massacre' (1993)
Philbens, Dr. Hugh; 'Hungerford- A Pictorial History' (1992)
Rawlinson, Peter, (Rt. Hon, Lord Rawlinson of Ewell, P.C. QC); 'A Price too High' (1989)
Roberts, Cecil, 'And so to Bath' (1940).
Rose, Geoffrey; 'A Pictorial History of the Oxford City Police' (1979)
Williams, Montague; 'Leaves of my Life' (1890)
Oxford City Police Occurrence Book (1869-1870)

ACKNOWLEDGEMENTS

I have been helped tremendously in the preparation of this book and everyone I have approached has willingly written, listened, offered advice and generally gone out of their way to help me. To those people I offer my grateful thanks, for without their help this book could never have been completed. First and foremost I would like to record my sincere appreciation to Mrs. Gillian Coward for all her help, understanding and encouragement. I would also like to thank Joe Coffey, lately of Thames Valley Police, who recalled the investigation into the murder of Ian Coward. To Richard Godfrey, ex-Chief Inspector, for not only sharing with me his article on the murders of Drewitt and Shorter published in the Police Review but for also taking time out to show me the scene of the crime and the memorial crosses erected to the Policemen.

To Inspector Bill Sandalls for his kind permission to photograph Hungerford Police Station and ex Sergeant Brian Tagg for his assistance at that station. I would like to record also my thanks to Sue Healey, lately curator of the Thames Valley Police Museum at Sulhamstead for all her help in the preparation of this book and to Ken Wells, who now occupies that post. Also to Tom Nichol, John Ryan and other members of the Thames Valley Police Welfare Section for their assistance. John Allen of Hungerford was most helpful with the history and records of nineteenth century Hungerford as was Dr. Philbens, also of that town, who allowed me to use a photograph of the tollhouse from his book on Hungerford. I would also like to record my appreciation of the assistance given me by Sergeant Anthony Rae of the Lancashire Constabulary and to Bob Dobson, a retired officer of that force, for allowing me to refer to his history of the Lancashire Constabulary. Geoffrey Rose, former Sergeant in the Thames Valley Police and author of the history of the Oxford City Police, willingly assisted me with the Gilkes killing. Also Peter Stowe and David Smith, who are great nephews of Joseph Gilkes, and who were able to provide me with a photograph of their great uncle, whilst he served briefly, with the Metropolitan Police. The staff of the Berkshire Record Office, Newbury Reference Library, Reading Reference Library, Oxfordshire Record Office and the Newspaper Library, Colindale were of great help to me in the research. Steve Spencer, of the Royal Borough of Windsor and Maidenhead Leisure and Culture Dept., was most helpful in locating the sadly unmarked grave of Inspector East and his widow. Mrs. Ethel Newynskyj of Harwell kindly allowed me to photograph her house, formerly The Chequers public house, where P.C. Charlton was killed in 1899 and Harold Connolly also of Harwell who produced photographs of The Chequers public house as it was at the turn of the century. William 'Bill' Boughton, retired Detective Chief Inspector of the Oxfordshire/Thames Valley Constabularies, was most helpful in detailing the investigation into the Inspector Bradley killing, as was Tony Walton, formerly a Detective Constable of the Thames Valley Police with his recollections of the so called Hungerford massacre. I owe a great debt of gratitude to Inspector Paul Brightwell of the Thames Valley Police who spent many hours going through the 'siege' of Hungerford with me and gave me so much advice concerning that terrible day.

Finally to my wife Mary for all her help during the research and preparation of this book.

PREFACE

The killing of a Police Officer in this country has always been a fairly unusual event and when one is murdered on duty the matter is given, as it should be, great coverage on television, in the newspapers and on the wireless. This is, in my belief, right and proper, not only because a man or, increasingly nowadays, a woman officer has lost his or her life but because, generally, that Police Officer has been on duty without being armed with a gun, as he or she would be in virtually every other country in the world. Whether this would be any different if the Police were armed is a matter of conjecture and one which society in this country will have to address if it becomes increasingly more violent. Out of all the Police Forces in the United Kingdom, I have taken one, the Thames Valley Police, which was formed in 1968 and comprises the counties of Berkshire, Buckinghamshire and Oxfordshire, and written the story of the Policemen who have been killed on duty as a result of criminal action. I have taken events from 1869 up to modern times and they nearly all arise from chance encounters with members of the public as the Policemen involved went about their work. The only one who was on a specific assignment was the last, Police Constable Brereton, sent to Hungerford in 1987 specifically in response to a number of calls from members of the public. All were unarmed, except for the small truncheon they carried, if they were in fact carrying them at the time of the incidents described.

The several forces which policed the area now known as the Thames Valley Police District were formed from 1835 onwards with, initially, the passing of the Municipal Corporations Act of that year which allowed a number of forces to be created in towns such as Reading, Buckingham, Maidenhead etc. The County and Borough Police Act of 1856 next compelled the counties to form their own Constabularies, hence Berkshire, Buckinghamshire and Oxfordshire. These were gradually whittled down over the years until 1968 when the five forces still remaining were amalgamated into the Thames Valley Constabulary, (later renamed Thames Valley Police).

In the one hundred and seventy years since the formation of the first forces eight Policemen have been killed within the Thames Valley area (I am excluding those who have died as a result of an accident or have been killed by enemy air raids). I am hopeful, of course, that is the complete and final list.

One further point intrigued me; of the eight deaths I have narrated, six occurred within the County of Berkshire, three in one town, Hungerford; the other two happened in Oxfordshire whilst none have been murdered in Buckinghamshire. I can offer no conclusions on that.

"IF YOU DON'T GO, I WILL PUT YOU OFF!"

POLICE CONSTABLE JOSEPH GILKES
Oxford City Police - 1869

The (new) Oxford City Police commenced duty on Friday, 1st January 1869 and would be the last of the various Police Forces formed before the creation of the Thames Valley Constabulary ninety-nine years later. The newly formed force took over authority for the city under the terms of the Oxford City Police Act, 1868. There were few Police forces that could boast their own specific Act of Parliament as their genesis. Generally, boroughs or city forces were brought about by the Town Police Clauses Act of 1835 and the county constabularies by virtue of the various County Police Acts of the mid-nineteenth century.

Such was the rush to have the 'new ' Police out on the streets of Oxford that they were initially unable to be issued with uniform and wore an on duty armlet on the sleeve of their coats as the only indication of who or what they were.[1]

There were between 25 to 30 men appointed to the new force with Charles Head, late of the Metropolitan Police, as its Superintendent.[2] Other members of the new force had also served with the Metropolitan Police, the Oxfordshire Constabulary or the previous Oxford Police. Some were entirely new to the Police.[3] The force had only been in existence for one month when it was confronted with its first tragedy.

On the evening of Thursday, 4th February, Police Constable Joseph Hilary Gilkes, aged 22 years, a native of Great Rollright, and Police Constable Francis Wilkes were in Blackfriars Road in the city. Gilkes had originally joined the Metropolitan Police in 1868 where his brother, Thomas was already serving, and had then transferred to the Oxford City Police.[4]

---

1 'A Pictorial History of the Oxford City Police.' Geoffrey Rose, 1979.
2 In mid-Victorian times, Superintendent or Head Constable was the preferred title for the Chief Officer of a borough or city Police. The Home Office frowned on the use of the term Chief Constable for other than a County force. 3 Rose. 4 Rose, and letter from peter Stowe, great nephew of Gilkes.

1

P.C. Joseph Hilary Gilkes (Oxford City Police)

The two men came upon a crowd of men and women outside Axtell's butcher's shop waiting for cheap cuts of meat and apparently causing an obstruction. Instructions to the Police were quite explicit about this. Any Constable encountering a crowd was to disperse it and render the paths clear for passers-by. Therefore, when he confronted this mob of people along the pavement, Joseph Gilkes saw his duty quite plainly and he ordered them, in a somewhat peremptory manner, to clear the path to allow other persons to use it freely. The fact that he was not in uniform, or questionably whether he was actually on duty, did not arise in Gilkes' mind. He knew what he had to do and he intended to carry out what he saw as his responsibilities. He instructed the persons gathered around the shop to move.

One of the crowd, Mrs. Keziah Cox, a tailor's wife, upon seeing a man in ordinary, civilian clothes ordering her and others about, enquired if Gilkes was a Police Officer.

Curtly the Constable retorted that it was,"...no odds to her." And once more he requested that she "move on."

To assist her on her way, Gilkes gave her a shove. It was by all accounts not too violent a push but unfortunately Mrs. Cox slipped and fell. Rising, she commenced using bad language towards the Police Officer and then hit him with her hand. Keziah's husband now came up and also began battering Gilkes, knocking him to the ground. Gilkes pulled himself up, only to be struck another blow by Mrs. Cox, who battered him about the head with a dish she was holding, breaking the dish in two as she did so.

Several others in the crowd, which apparently numbered in the region of sixty persons, began to shout at the unfortunate Policeman. Mrs. Cox's brother, James Blay, asked to see Gilkes' authority (warrant card) and started pulling him about. One man, emboldened by the crowd, was heard to shout, "Give it him! He deserves it!"

Mrs. Cox, not to be outdone, threw pieces of the broken dish at the Constable.

Gilkes must by now have realised that he would be in dire trouble if he remained where he was, and decided that flight was his only option. His companion, Wilkes, had been conspicuous by his absence whilst all this turmoil had been taking place (he would be called to account later for his inaction). As Gilkes ran off, the mob, now thoroughly incensed, chased after him.

The Constable was pursued to the River Isis [5] and, seeing no alternative, jumped in, in an effort to escape the clutches of the howling crowd. The swift flowing river carried him away.

The Superintendent of Police was informed and a search was made for Gilkes. A waterman later recovered the body of the Constable and conveyed the corpse to the Nag's Head in Bridport Street.

Mr. and Mrs. Cox meanwhile were arrested in The Forester's Arms by Police Constables White and Hamlett and were brought before an Inquest convened the next day.

A John Scarrott was one of the first to give evidence. He said that he had seen a man in the crowd without a hat being pushed about by people. Scarrott had heard him say that he was a Policeman but he had not been wearing a Police uniform. He had also heard the Policeman tell the woman to move on and then there would be no bother. She had retorted that she wanted to know his name as she wished to report him for pushing her down. When the crowd started to hiss him, Gilkes had started to walk away. Scarrott had also seen Blay come up and start pulling him about and then, when the Policeman had run off, people had chased after him, whilst Mrs. Cox had thrown bits of her broken plate at him.

The next witness said that he had seen Gilkes being struck by a girl of fifteen. The Policeman had just come up and ordered the crowd to move. He understood that Gilkes had told the crowd that he was a Special Constable.

Another related that there had been no row until the Policeman had arrived on the scene. He did admit however that there were rather more people there than usual.

5 *Whilst it runs through Oxford, the River Thames is known as the Isis.*

A further witness said that complaints had been made about the numbers on the footpath.

Constable Francis Wilkes was listened to quite attentively as he now gave evidence. He lived in Speedwell Street, St. Ebbes, he informed the Inquest, and Gilkes had been lodging at his house. On the previous evening, he, Wilkes, had been walking along Commercial Road with Gilkes intending, he said, to go and purchase some meat from Axtell's shop. They had both been off duty and in plain clothes. They had seen a number of persons collected together and they had asked them what they wanted. Gilkes had said, "What do you want here? You had better go on. You must not stop the road up." Wilkes heard someone reply, "I won't go!" His colleague had then responded, "If you don't go, I will put you off!" Gilkes had pushed Mrs. Cox off the footpath, without, he thought, using unnecessary violence. Mrs Cox had then struck his colleague, with both hands and with the dish, about his head.

The Coroner was most heedful of what Wilkes had to say. When the Constable had finished he commented, "It is most extraordinary that the witness Wilkes should stand by and see a brother Constable injured in the way he had done. To say nothing of his duty as an Englishman to help a fellow man from being attacked."

Wilkes attempted to justify himself by saying that there had been seventy persons at the scene. If he had interfered, he might have been attacked as his comrade had been.

Wilkes was replaced by Henry Lundon who now gave evidence. He had been coming out of a public house when he had noticed Gilkes running away and people shouting out after him, "Stop that thief!" Lundon had called out to Gilkes, "Stop, my good man. Nobody shall hurt you."

Gilkes had replied, "I cannot. If I do they'll kill me!" Lundon acknowledged that Gilkes appeared to be in a terrible fright.

Someone saw the Policeman either stumble or spring into the river. His contribution to the saga was to call out to Gilkes, "What do you want in the water? Nobody is going to hurt you." He seemed quite put out when Gilkes made no reply.

When Gilkes' body had been recovered from the Isis, George Taunton had 'inspected' it and observed that there were two scalp wounds on the back of the head such as might have been inflicted by blows from a dish or plate. The skull had not been broken and he believed that death had been due to drowning.

The Coroner now summed up. He did not think there was sufficient evidence to justify the jury in returning a verdict of manslaughter. The evidence appeared to him to lead to the conclusion that Gilkes was drowned but from the circumstances related that he had taken the wrong turn and had gone into the water at a time when rescue was impossible. On the other hand, he continued, if the members of the jury were of the opinion that Gilkes was so terrified that his death was caused by fear, the party would be guilty of the crime of manslaughter.

The jury considered the matter for half an hour and returned saying that Joseph Gilkes was drowned whilst endeavouring to escape from Kezia Cox, her husband and Blay who had violently assaulted him. The foreman also requested that, as an accident had previously occurred at the same place the attention of the local board should be directed to it so that a fence might be erected. The Coroner agreed.

In April Mr. and Mrs. Cox were charged with 'savagely assaulting' the Constable before the City Quarter Sessions.

Police Constable Wilkes was pointedly asked why he had not assisted his colleague during the fracas. He replied, somewhat lamely, "Because I thought that I was not required."

After hearing similar evidence to that at the Inquest, the Recorder commented that there was no case against John Cox. His wife had been knocked down by Gilkes. The prosecutors were however quite right in bringing the case into Court because it must be shown that persons could not be molested, as Gilkes had been with impunity. With the woman, however, it was a case of excess in the amount of her violence for which she would be liable, picking up pieces of dish and throwing them at the Constable.

John Cox was therefore acquitted whilst his wife, having been found guilty, was sentenced to be imprisoned for seven days.

The question remains; had Gilkes been killed whilst on duty? Wilkes, in his evidence, as reported in all the Oxford newspapers, said that both he and Gilkes had been off duty and in plain clothes and fetching some meat from Axtell's shop. When Gilkes saw the crowd gathered outside the shop he may have considered that it was his duty to move them on, especially as people were complaining about the numbers. Therefore he may have attempted to use his authority, as a recently sworn in member of the 'new' Oxford Police, to get them to form a more orderly queue. There appears no question that he informed the crowd that he was a Policeman and he might even have been wearing an 'on duty' armlet, although he was in civilian clothes.

An entry in the Oxford City Police Occurrence Book covering the event, stated that Wilkes returned to his lodgings in St. Ebbes after he had seen his comrade run off.

It was and can still be quite hazardous attempting to move a crowd of people on who are causing an obstruction, and several Policemen in the nineteenth century died from injuries received doing just that. It would appear that Gilkes certainly died as a result of being attacked whilst acting as a Policeman.

As for Police Constable Wilkes, he, not surprisingly, resigned from the Force.

"....NO MORE HORRIBLE OUTRAGE HAS BEEN COMMITTED."

INSPECTOR JOSEPH DREWITT &
POLICE CONSTABLE THOMAS SHORTER
Berkshire Constabulary 1876

PART ONE

"It is my most painful duty to report that Inspector Joseph Drewitt and P.C. Shorter were brutally murdered on the Hungerford and Wantage Turnpike Road on the night of December 11th last. Four men are in custody charged with their murders who, without doubt, uttered threats against them but unfortunately such evidence cannot be received against them. I have recommended that the widow of the late Inspector Drewitt be granted the full amount of gratuity sanctioned by the Act of Parliament with one year's pay. The late Inspector served seventeen years, four months in the Berkshire Constabulary and bore an exemplary record. Unfortunately, the Act of Parliament does not authorise any gratuity to the widow of a Constable who has not contributed to the superannuation for three years and inasmuch as P.C. 46 Thomas Shorter had only served two years in the force I am precluded from recommending his widow for a gratuity. P.C.Shorter was a most promising Constable and bore a high character.

Aggravated and other assaults on the Police are on the increase. Only last quarter two persons were convicted of brutal assaults on Constables and four are charged with murder and eleven persons have been summarily convicted this quarter of assaults on Constables."

Thus did Colonel Adam Blandy, the Chief Constable of Berkshire report to the Justices at the County Quarter Sessions[1] on 1st January 1877 on one of the blackest days in the one hundred and twelve year history of the Berkshire Constabulary.

---

[1] *The Police Committee for County Police forces until the Local Government Act 1888 created Standing Joint Committees.*

BRUTAL MURDER!!
In Berkshire.

On Monday, December 11th, Inspector Drewitt, and P. C. Shorter were found murdered on the high road, one mile from Hungerford. Four desperate Poachers are in custody for the crime.

Tune—Driven from Home.

A barbarous murder on the country road side,
All throughout Berkshire is spread far and wide,
An Inspector of police, and a private as well,
Both have been murdered, we're sorry to tell.
Upon Monday night their bodies were found
By another Policeman on his lonely round ;
When near Dewford toll-bar a sight met his gaze,
He'll never forget to the end of his days.

CHORUS.

Near Hungerford, in Berkshire, on a lonely road
side,
Two Policemen by a murder so cruel they died ;
Quite dead and cold they were both of them found,
Their brains beaten out as they lay on the ground.

A more unmanly crime has seldom been known,
I am sure you will say if your hearts are not stone,
To take poor men's lives in cold blood we must say,
Is not like an Englishman' love of fair play ;
They must have been beaten to death on the ground,
Till the blood of the victims in pools lay around !
They gave them no chance their lives to defend,
The unequall struggle soon came to an end.

The eleventh of December, a dark gloomy night,
The two men were found, what a sad ghastly sight !
By the police of the district the alarm was soon
spread,
Much sympathy was shown for the poor murdered
dead.

Four men were taken with blood on their clothes,
Whether they are guilty God only knows !
We will not condemn, tho' they bear a bad name,
f they are the murderers so much to their shame.

Two of the men who are taken, they say,
Must have passed down the road where the two
bodies lay ;
The man at the toll gate saw them go through.
He watch'd for their coming as had been told to do ;
They seem'd agitated and hurried along,
Suspicion against them has been very strong ;
Let us take care that none but the guilty shall fall,
Tho' this world's full of trouble, life's dear to us all.

Four men are charged with this cruel crime,
The charge they must answer at the proper time ;
Two men have been killed, and justice will say,
The murderers we know cannot be far away.
Blood for blood has long been the law of the land,
And in crimes that are done with a cowardly hand,
It is nothing but right such men should be taught
The revenge of a murderer is too dearly bought.

These Policemen, no doubt, have left children and
wives,
Who are plunged in a sorrow that will last them
their lives ;
They will never forget where'er they may roam,
The night when they brought these poor murdered
men home.
Their prospects in future are blighted and gone,
We hope they're not friendless altho' they're alone,
As they stand by the grave of those they love best,
May their prayers be heard for the dear ones at rest.

London :—H. P. SUCH, Machine Printer and Publisher, 177, Union-street, Borough.

Ballad commemorating the murders of Inspector Drewitt and Constable Shorter

Inspector Joseph Drewitt (Berkshire Constabulary)

P.C. Thomas Shorter (Berkshire Constabulary)

For the British Police as a whole the decade from 1871 to 1880 was an extremely bloody one. It has been estimated that twenty-six Police Officers were either killed or died of the injuries they received whilst on duty. In one year alone, 1876, five Policemen were murdered. (These figures have only been equalled once since, in the violent 1980s.)[2]

In that particular year, 1876, Joseph Drewitt was in charge of the Police in the west Berkshire town of Hungerford and for the surrounding area. He had been promoted to the rank of Inspector and had been posted to the town in April. He was married and with his wife and five children lived above the Police Station.

Hungerford Police Station from where Inspector Drewitt set out on his last patrol.

In the early part of December he had organised a collection for the family of a Somerset Policeman who had been killed by a gang of men the previous month. Whilst making enquiries in the area in an effort to trace the killers who had temporarily made good their escape, Inspector Drewitt had made the chance remark to the town stationmaster that, similar to railway accidents, outrages like the

2 A. Rae.

12

murder of Police Officers closely followed each other. He had then added that he did not think there was anyone in the Hungerford area evil enough to commit such a deed as the recent murder in Somerset.[3]

A few days later, on the evening of Monday 11th December, Inspector Drewitt left the Police Station to visit his men on their night patrols. The hours worked by the Police in the Victorian era were long and arduous. The Constables, especially the country beat officers, usually patrolled three or four hours by day, had a break and resumed at night for the remainder of their shift. It was truly said that a Policeman rarely finished duty on the same day that he had started and there were no rest days as of right.

The Constables patrolling their lonely country beats could expect to be visited by a supervisory Officer, either a Sergeant or Inspector, at a 'conference point' during the course of their tour of duty.[4]

Drewitt strolled along the High Street under the Great Western Railway Bridge and the first Policeman that he met by the Bear Hotel was P.C. William Isaacs of the Wiltshire Constabulary[5]. After a rather long conversation, Isaacs was to say later that Drewitt had met him at

*The Bear, Hungerford, where Drewitt met a fellow Constable
shortly before being murdered. (As it is today)*

3 *This was the killing of P.C. Cox for which three men were eventually charged.*
4 *This was an arranged place where a Constable could be visited by any of his supervisory officers. To omit to make a 'point', unless the Constable had a very good reason, was a disciplinary offence.*
5 *The County boundary of Wiltshire came closer to the town in the nineteenth century.*

9.30pm and did not leave until 10.10pm. The Inspector finished by saying that he was walking to the toll gate to meet P.C.Shorter at his point. The two men parted, walking off in opposite directions. Sometime after this encounter P.C. Isaacs heard the sound of a gun being discharged in the distance.

Thomas Shorter, whom Drewitt intended meeting, was the Constable on the Great Shefford beat and he had been making his way from that village to his appointment with his Inspector at the toll gate. He had been seen, trudging the four lonely miles from Great Shefford to the rendezvous, by the occupier of a cottage at Hungerford New Town, John Green. Twenty minutes later Green heard the report of a gun then, sometime after, another. The first he reckoned came from the toll gate area further down the road whilst the second appeared to have come from nearby Piggott's Farm.

It was about this time that P.C.William Golby left Hungerford Police Station on his tour of duty. His instructions were to meet Inspector Drewitt at the junction of the Bath Road with the Wantage Road, Folly Hill, before he, Golby, left the town.

P.C. Golby must have been somewhat mystified therefore when the Inspector failed to meet him and so, knowing that Drewitt had gone to see the Great Shefford Constable, Golby set off along the Wantage Road hoping to encounter Drewitt as that officer returned towards Hungerford from making contact with P.C. Shorter.

As Golby walked along the lonely road with the trees and hedges on either side making it seem all the more dark and forbidding, (according to witnesses it was, at the time a clear night; later on it started to rain) he noticed something lying in the road. At first, taking it to be a drunken man, he prodded the prostrate body with his night-stick.[6] There was no response and Golby stooped down to examine the man more closely. Putting his hand out, his fingers touched something warm and soft. Intrigued, Golby struck a match and saw that it was the body of a Policeman! Alarmed, he now lit his

---

6 On night duty Police Officers were issued with a stout walking stick for protection. This was in addition to the truncheon they carried, usually secreted.

P.C. William Golby (Berkshire Constabulary)

bulls-eye lantern and casting the light over the body was horrified to discover that it was in fact his colleague, P.C.Shorter, and a pitiable sight it was too for he had been subjected to a ferocious attack. The Policeman's head had been battered and parts of his skull lay as much as a foot and a half away from his body. With a shudder, Golby realised that the softness he had felt as he had knelt down had been P.C. Shorter's brains, spewed out along the lane.

Golby was now in an appalling situation. He was on his own in a dark country lane by the body of a very recently slain Policeman with the distinct possibility that the killers were still in the vicinity and therefore watching his every move; maybe even at this very moment poised behind the hedge, ready to attack and even murder him. His ears picked up every sudden rustle in the undergrowth and any stirring must now have assumed in the lonely Constable's mind a most frightening aspect. Were they the usual noises that anyone who walked abroad at night would casually dismiss as the movements of nocturnal animals scurrying about on their multifarious tasks? Or were they the stirrings of the assassins of P.C. Shorter, positioning themselves even as Golby looked carefully around, with the light from his lantern, ready to leap from their hiding place and deal out the same to him as they had done to his comrade? Golby must have tightened his grip on his nightstick just in case he was attacked.

As if that was not enough, another worrying thought must have occurred to him. If Drewitt had arranged to meet P.C. Shorter at his point and that Constable was now lying dead at Golby's feet, where now was the Inspector? A man placed in such an unenviable position as this must have had nerves of steel not to have panicked.

The sound of the Hungerford Town clock striking in the distance brought Golby back to reality. He stood up and walked to the Eddington tollgate on the Wantage Road and roused the keeper, William Hedges, and his wife. Explaining what had occurred Golby instructed them to keep a lookout for anyone who came past whilst he returned to Hungerford to seek assistance.

Eddington Turnpike Gate

Shortly after P.C. Golby had left the scene, the toll-keeper saw two men approaching. Hedges and his wife knew them both very well; William Day and William Tidbury who lived further along the road. Hedges greeted them, "Well Bill!", to which they replied, "Well Bill."

Tidbury then remarked to the toll-keeper's wife, "How you do shiver." Mrs. Hedges answered, "Yes and so do you."

When Hedges also commented that the two men appeared to be shivering they replied that they had been standing about. Day and Tidbury walked off in the direction of their homes. After a few yards however Hedges noticed that the two men broke into a run.

When Golby reached Hungerford he obtained a horse and cart and with some of the townsfolk returned to the scene of the murder and loaded P.C. Shorter's body onto the conveyance. As they moved the corpse it was noticed that it had been lying on top of a gunlock, still wet with the Constable's blood. Later, when it was examined more carefully, it was seen that the screw, which would have fastened it to the stock of the gun, appeared to have been recently broken.

Folly Cross Roads, where two policemen were murdered.

Golby took P.C. Shorter's body to The Lancaster Arms in the town then met P.C. Brown, the Constable from Kintbury (a parish approximately four miles from Hungerford). It was by now 1.30am and Golby informed him of the murder of their fellow Policeman. He asked if Brown had seen Inspector Drewitt as he had been due to meet him after visiting Shorter and Golby. "No," was the firm reply. Both men now began the search for their Officer in the rather forlorn hope that they might find him alive and well.

As the Constables commenced their search with the light from their bulls eye lanterns sweeping the country lanes, their task was not made any more agreeable as rain, steady and relentless, now began to fall.

After reaching the tollgate, the two Policemen separated, Brown wandering down Gypsy Lane whilst Golby walked along Denford Lane. A few minutes later P.C. Brown heard a shout from Golby. He had discovered Inspector Drewitt lying by the side of the lane. As P.C.Golby shone his lantern over the body he knew instinctively that his superior officer was beyond all human aid. "His head," he was to

Scene of Inspector Drewitt's murder. (As it is today)

Scene of P.C. Shorter's murder. (As it is today)

recount later, "was battered to pieces and his brains lay upon the grass." The Inspector's body lay approximately 150 yards from where that of P.C.Shorter's had been discovered.

Looking cautiously around in case the murderers of the two Policemen were still lurking about, Goldby could see that someone had broken through the hedge near to where Drewitt lay, something he had also noticed at the scene of Shorter's murder. When he had time to examine the place more thoroughly it appeared to him that two men had passed through. Something else occurred to the Constable, the attack on the two Policemen had obviously been so sudden that neither of them had had time to draw their truncheons to defend themselves.

Golby told Brown to remain at the scene whilst he made a second melancholy walk to Hungerford to fetch a suitable conveyance for the removal of the Inspector's body. On his return he found that a farmer passing by had offered the use of his cart to P.C. Brown and the men carefully lifted the corpse on to it, picking up his uniform cap that lay close by and, incidentally, finding another cap which had been lying under the Inspector, which they also retrieved. The two Constables marched into Hungerford and placed the body of Inspector Drewitt alongside that of P.C. Shorter.

Golby had already seen that a message had been relayed to Superintendent George Bennett at the Divisional Headquarters at Newbury apprising him of the night's ghastly events. That officer hastily made his way to The Lancaster Arms where, after viewing the bodies which were laid out in the coach-house and having been briefed by P.C.Golby, he now commenced his enquiries. Suspicion immediately fell upon certain members of a disreputable family who lived a little way out of Hungerford. They were William Tidbury, aged 24, Henry, or Harry Tidbury, 26, Francis, or Frank Tidbury, 17 and William Day, 38, who was related to them by marriage, his daughter having married William Tidbury. Both William Tidbury and his wife lived with Mr and Mrs Day. Harry lived in an adjoining cottage and Frank still resided with his parents close by. All were well known to the Police.

Bennett had his suspicions confirmed when he heard of the encounter the Hedges had had with Day and his son-in-law during the night and taking a number of Policemen with him went to apprehend the suspected murderers.

It was by now 7am and as the posse of Police arrived they found only Day still at home, the others having gone to work. When he was informed that he was being arrested on suspicion of murder, Day replied, "I know nothing about it. I went up to Mr Piggott's last night with Bill Tidbury to plug in an engine and on our way back when we got to the toll-bar we saw a man or something lying by the road-side. We thought it was somebody drunk. We did not stay to see who it was." He added that he had reached his home by the road whilst Bill Tidbury had come across the fields and they had met at the tollgate. (He was later to elaborate upon this before the Magistrates.)

A search was conducted of Day's cottage and a gun was found standing in a corner which appeared to have been recently fired, with an exploded cap on the nipple. The Police also discovered an empty powder flask and a bag containing mixed shot and another bag holding gunpowder. These items were all seized.

Superintendent Bennett next went to the Eddington Iron Works, where Harry and Frank worked, and detained them both. Harry's response was, "I am innocent. I know nothing about it." Frank answered, "I know nothing about. I wasn't there." Bennett picked up this off-hand remark and commented to a bystander, "You hear what he says, 'I wasn't there.' Yet I had mentioned no place!"

It now remained to apprehend the last one of the Tidburys and he was found working on a farm at Kintbury. When he was first arrested he declared that he knew nothing about the murders and that he had been in bed by 9pm. "Oh," said the Superintendent, "I was informed you passed through Eddington gate after 10pm!"

Realising that he had been caught out in a lie, Bill Tidbury was forced to admit, "Yes, I and my father-in-law had been up to Piggott's Farm to put a plug in an engine and when we went through Eddington Gate we saw Bill Hedges and his wife and never saw anyone else."

All the captured men were taken, initially, to Hungerford Police Station.

According to the local newspapers, which were much freer in their comments than they would be nowadays, the prisoners were well known in the district for their 'wild ways' and it was quoted in one paper, that, 'all the men are poachers and with the exception of Francis have been before the magistrates.' Day was reported as being, 'a somewhat notorious character and has been more or less feared and suspected in the neighbourhood.'

It was now 8.45am and Superintendent Bennett, having lodged his prisoners, went about gathering further evidence. In this he was not only assisted by members of his own force but by several officers from the adjoining Wiltshire Constabulary. Bennett went to the scene of the murders. A man had found P.C. Shorter's helmet lying on the other side of the hedge close to where his body had been found and it was handed over to the Superintendent. When Bennett compared the hammer of the gun taken from Day's cottage with the indentations found on the helmet he formed the opinion that they corresponded exactly. He also thought that the butt of the gun fitted a hole in the helmet.

A passer-by had seen a cord lying a few yards from the Constable's body and gave this to Bennett as well. Bennett was to show this to Bill Tidbury (Snr), who alleged that it belonged to Day whilst others, to whom it was shown, thought that it had been used by Day at his place of employment. It smelt strongly of lard oil, which apparently was used with threshing machines. Someone else believed that he had seen Day using it when he was engaged in ferreting.

Bennett now moved on to where Drewitt's body had lain. A

tobacco box was found near the body and in an adjoining field there was a trigger plate smeared with blood. Bennett also noticed that there were some very distinct boot marks leading from the site of the murder to the rear of the Tidburys' cottages and which, when he came to look more closely at the boots worn by the prisoners, appeared to him to be of a similar pattern.

Sergeant Bull of the Wiltshire Constabulary thought so as well and noted that other boot marks he had found, including one in some cow dung, matched Frank Tidbury's boots. He also believed that, from the length of the stride, the men who had left the marks behind had been running.

The clothing that the four prisoners had been wearing was taken from them and was looked at carefully and later sent for more detailed scientific examination, although Bennett was satisfied that they were bloodstained and that attempts had been made to remove those stains by the application of red lead which the prisoners had access to at their place of employment.

The shot taken from Day's cottage was compared with that from the body of Inspector Drewitt. Both samples were of mixed shot and Bennett believed that they corresponded.

Witnesses were traced who could give the movements of the Tidburys and Day on the night of the murders. One could say that he had met the Tidburys about 7pm coming out of the lane below the Turnpike gate and saw them go up the hill where they were met by Day.

A servant at nearby Hidden Farm, Elizabeth King, stated that Day and Bill Tidbury were at the farm at about 8pm that night and had used red lead whilst they were working and candles to see what they were doing. She had orders, she said from her 'master', to give them two quarts of ale. She remembered Day remarking that he wished she would hurry up as he did not want to be there half the night having another job in store.

Elizabeth Bryant, who lived in a cottage with her father at Prickett's

Lot, which was only two minutes from where Inspector Drewitt's body had been found, told the Police that she had been in Hungerford until 10pm. that Monday when she had returned to her cottage with her father. When she had walked back from Hungerford she had not seen anything in the road, she said. However, when she had gone to the rear of the cottage before going to bed she had heard at least two men, maybe more, pass by. She had heard them talking and although she could not make out most of what they were saying she did hear one of them mention seeing a light.

John Hancox, the foreman of the foundry where the Tidburys worked, was shown the cap found by the body of Inspector Drewitt and he was adamant that it belonged to Henry Tidbury. He had, he asserted, seen him wear it " hundreds of times" and recognised it by the grease on it and a button on the side. Hancox added that Henry had been wearing a billycock hat when he had turned up for work on the morning following the murders. He had appeared agitated and pale and had made some comment to Hancox about the murders. He had asked if he could go and look at the scene but the foreman had told him to go about his work.

At the request of the Police Mr. Hancox assisted them in obtaining wax impressions of the boot marks that had been found near where the murders had taken place; apparently Superintendent Bennett wanted an independent witness when he took the impressions which would later be produced as evidence in Court.

When news of the murders reached the outside world there was widespread revulsion that such a heinous crime had been enacted. The local newspapers were unanimous in their condemnation of such a vile crime.

The Newbury Weekly News, in its editorial, commented,"Seldom has it been our melancholy task to chronicle a crime so atrocious as the sickening details which will be found in our columns today...but the wanton sacrifice of two useful lives destroyed with circumstances of unusual brutality and apparently without adequate motive to prompt the deed has justly evoked the universal outburst of sorrow and indignation...An outraged society will demand that a terrible example will be made of those ruffians who have wantonly destroyed two public servants whose very office as preservers of the peace renders this the more obligatory that the violation of that personal safety should be effectively vindicated.'

The Reading Observer declared,' Two of the foulest and most brutal murders of modern times have this week been committed in our county. The quieter rural district of Hungerford has been the theatre of the awful tragedy and two honourable and efficient public servants have been the victims in the prime of life and in the faithful discharge of their arduous and reasonable duties... Drewitt and Shorter have been foully and brutally murdered by a gang of lawless poachers.... there is literally nothing to mitigate the hideous depravity which it reveals...'

'One of the most cowardly and diabolical outrages ever committed upon the Police of this county was perpetrated within a few minutes walk of the town on Monday night,' thundered the Reading Mercury, whilst on the national scene The Daily Telegraph considered the murders '...a dreadful outrage.' The Daily Chronicle added, 'Shocking murder of two Police Officers by poachers...'The Times merely commented,'Colonel Blandy, the Chief Constable, reached Hungerford about mid-day yesterday, 12th December and proceeded immediately to the scene which was visited by hundreds of excited people during the morning.'

The Inquest was opened on 15th December and the Town Clerk, after swearing in the jury, referred to the sad occurrence that had brought them together. "Probably no more horrible outrage has been committed in this district for years," he added.

Then, the members of the jury were taken to the coach-house of The Lancaster Arms where they viewed the bodies of the two dead Policemen. The reporter of the Reading Observer also attended and described the scene for his readers; 'The spectacle which here presented itself was a most ghastly one. The deceased, who were dressed in overcoats buttoned up, were lying on straw side by side. Both were in the same condition as when found. Their faces were covered with blood and their heads were so frightfully battered that their brains protruded. The deceased were well known to most of the jury and the features were readily recognised by them.'

The jury, their gruesome task over, returned to the Courtroom and listened as Superintendent Bennett formally identified the bodies.

P.C. Golby had just given his evidence when Colonel Blandy intervened and requested that the Inquest be adjourned as no detailed post-mortems had been performed and, although a great deal of evidence had been collected, the case was not yet completed. A local practitioner, Dr.Major, confirmed that he had only carried out a superficial examination and an adjournment was agreed to, pending the autopsies being performed.

When the Inquest was resumed, Dr.Major gave the result of the post mortems. He had, he declared, examined Drewitt's body and had found that he had sustained a large wound to the right hand side of his throat into which he could insert three fingers. This injury had been 'plugged up' with the inside lining of the coat that Drewitt had been wearing on the night and was full of shot. He had extracted forty pellets from the wound and this injury alone would have caused the immediate death of the Inspector. In addition there was a clear break of six inches in Drewitt's skull and his brain was lacerated.

With P.C. Shorter he had noted that there were various bruises about his body and the Constable's head had been broken into twelve pieces and most of his brain had gone. His skull had been broken by repeated blows from a heavy instrument and in his opinion death would not have been so instantaneous as with Drewitt.

Other witnesses were brought forward and heard by the Coroner and the jury, who at the end of the day brought in a verdict of wilful murder against all the prisoners.

Colonel Adam Blandy - Chief Constable, Berkshire Constabulary.

<u>Harry Peter Major</u>, on his Oath Saith as follows:—

I am a Doctor of Medicine and General Practitioner practising in Hungerford — I examined the bodies of Inspector Joseph Drewett, and Police Constable Thomas Shorter on Tuesday the 12th of December instant — I first made an examination on the morning of that day at the "Lancaster Arms", in the Coach house there — I found the Skull and brains of both men so severely injured as to be sufficient to cause death — In the evening of the same day I made a more minute examination — I first examined the body of Inspector Drewett — I found no injuries on the trunk and lower extremities of Inspector Drewett — He was grazed on the middle of the left fore arm; there was a small punctured wound on the left elbow with everted edges, a small bruise in the middle of the left arm — My attention was next directed to a large circular opening on the right side of the neck, about an inch from the collar bone and two inches from the middle line of the throat — The edges were blackened, it was large enough to admit three fingers easily — I found this wound perfectly plugged with the wadding out of the Coat — I produce the wadding — It is the inside lining of the Coat — I found a great number of Shot mixed up with it — I took from the wound 40 shot which I produce — They appear to be mixed Shot — The direction of the wound was backwards and upwards to the base of the skull — I examined the skull and found the occipital bone severely fractured — The base

Post Mortem Report by Dr Major on bodies of Drewitt and Shorter.

of the brain was severely lacerated, and there was a large corresponding wound in the scalp, six inches in length, caused by the shot going out — I examined the scalp further forward, and about an inch from the other wound across the head from side to side, there was a Y shaped incision, about five inches in length, which did not communicate with the other scalp wound or the fracture — Across the crown of the head there was another incision of the scalp, about five inches in length, cut down to the bone, but no fracture there, and not connected with either of the others — These scalp wounds were caused by some other means than the shot — The shot wounds would have been instantaneously fatal — The two incised wounds were clean cut — From the direction of the shot wound I consider the barrel of the Gun was directed upwards — It must have been fired within six inches of the wound in the head — I have examined the Inspectors Clothes produced: the punctured wound in his left elbow was apparently a shot wound, but there is no corresponding perforation in the Coat — Inspector Druwitts Stock, inner and outer Coats produced have marks on the inside and outside corresponding with the wound in the neck — I afterwards examined the body of Police Constable Thomas Shorter, commencing my examination from below upwards — There was an extensive wound on the right groin 4 inches by 6 in size — There was a bruise on the scrotum, a small bruise underneath the Collar bone, the back of the left hand was badly bruised, the skin was knocked off the left little finger by the knuckle; there was a graze on the left side of the nose, effusion had taken place on both the upper eyelids, and they were blackened — I next directed my attention to the Skull: there were several scalp wounds, in most instances connected with fractures — Almost all the bones in the head were fractured — I removed twelve pieces, they were all either loose or separate; some of the bones removed were several inches in size; the right hemisphere of the brain was wanting — Some pieces of bone and brain were shewn to me in a bucket — I removed the other portion of the brain for the purpose of discovering whether there were any shot — I could find none, nor any indentation from shot — I consider that the fractures I have spoken of were caused by blows from some heavy instrument, and from the direction of the fractures, I consider the blows came from the top — There was a small punctured fracture at the junction of the left parietal and frontal bones; this I consider must have been caused by some pointed instrument — I consider the hammer of a Gun would be a very likely thing to have caused such a wound — The fractures and blows were quite sufficient to cause death; but I don't think the death of Shorter was nearly so instantaneous as that of Inspector Drewitt — I judge this from the greater effusion of blood and from the effusion on the eyelids — I think that many of the minor wounds on Shorter were inflicted before many of the severer ones, with the exception of the punctured wounds on the head before spoken of —

30

I consider that all the wounds were caused by some blunt instrument; the bruises on the groin and the state of the scrotum might have been caused by kicks – On the Thursday after the murder I examined the clothes of all the four Prisoners On examining the clothes of each prisoner and on the boots I found what I believe to be blood stains – On the clothes of some of the prisoners there were marks of red lead – On some of the clothes and more particularly on one Waistcoat I observed marks as if scraping had taken place – I also observed whitening or some kind of white powder on some of the clothes – Both Inspector Drewett and Police Constable Shorter were very powerful men.

The four men were taken to the Railway Station escorted by twenty Policemen, to be held at Police Stations other than Hungerford, as Colonel Blandy considered that lodging them there was inconsiderate, bearing in mind that Mrs Drewitt and her children were living in the same building.

A large crowd had gathered to see the prisoners as they were removed from the Inquest to the Station and they booed and hissed the alleged evildoers. Cries of, "Hang the villains!" were directed at them and it was only with the greatest difficulty that they were put on the train. Two of the accused were taken off at Newbury where another crowd awaited them as they were conveyed to the Police Station and a similar scene ensued at Reading where the remaining two were lodged in the cells of the County Police Station.[7]

The search for more evidence continued, urged on by the presence of the Chief Constable and in the garden at the rear of the Tidburys' cottages, two gun stocks were found, one of which had some

7 *Reading had its own borough Police Force at this time, quite separate from the County Constabulary.*

bloodstains on it, the other showing signs of having recently been broken off from the barrel a gun. The trigger plate, which had been found near the Inspector's body, fitted one of them exactly. The cottage where Frank Tidbury lived was also searched and an axe handle, which according to one newspaper reporter "..formed a most formidable bludgeon, the head of which is covered in blood" was located in an outhouse.

The accused were brought back to Hungerford as they had to appear before the Magistrates for the formal committal proceedings. 'None of the prisoners have the appearance of men likely to commit such a horrible deed' announced the Reading Observer. 'Day is short and rather stoutly built, has round features and slight whiskers and his countenance provides a kind of careless bravado expression.' Henry Tidbury was '...about medium height, slender build. He has very small features, short black whiskers and moustache.' Bill Tidbury was described as, 'taller and of more stalwart build. He has dark hair and whiskers,' whilst the youngest, Frank Tidbury, was, 'well built, has a fresh looking countenance and features.'

All the prisoners, the report went on,'...wore a careworn expression... Day and Henry Tidbury were very particularly dejected..' and 'Henry and William Tidbury had their eyes fixed on the ground throughout the greater part of the examination.'

The witnesses again went through their evidence and at the end of the proceedings the prisoners were asked if they had anything to say. Henry and Frank shook their heads but William Day and William Tidbury took the opportunity to speak up.

Day, in a long rambling statement, said that Bill Tidbury had arrived home early on the evening of 11th.December. He had asked him if he would go to Piggott's with him. He, Day, had left and had met Bill Tidbury at the farm where they had done some work. During the course of conversation he had told Day that he had come with his brothers, Harry and Frank, and they had gone to get a bird.

"I hope you harn't been meddlin' with my gun," he allegedly remarked to Bill Tidbury.

"No," the latter had replied. "I haven't touched it."

As they were working Day had heard the sound of two gunshots in the distance. They had finished their work at 10.15pm and Day had taken things back to the yard. When he returned Bill Tidbury had gone but as he was making his way back to his home on his own he had come across him. They had started walking together when Day had seen something lying in the road. "What's that there?" he had exclaimed and looked closer. "Why, it's a man or something."

Bill Tidbury had replied, "Come on, that's only someone drunk. Don't meddle with he." They had continued on their way but Day was not happy and wanted to return to the man lying in the road. Tidbury had dissuaded him from doing so however. They had passed Mr and Mrs Hedges and went home where they saw Henry Tidbury. Day had asked him if it was him that he had heard shooting earlier but he had denied doing so.

Next morning after Bill Tidbury had gone to work Henry had called at his, Day's, cottage and had spoken to Mrs Day, not realising that her husband was still about. He had asked her to tell her husband that if anyone was to ask if he had seen anything as he had come home the previous night he was to say 'No'. Day, who had not yet gone to work had heard this and had retorted that if he was asked he would say that he had seen somebody or something in the road. Henry had left and as Day was fastening his boots Superintendent Bennett had arrived. That was the first time, he asserted, that he had been aware that murder had been committed.

William Tidbury's statement was much more illuminating. After helping Day with the engine he had heard the sound of gunfire and, running across the footpath where he thought the sound had come from, he had eventually bumped into his brother Henry. "Did you hear I shoot?" Henry had asked his brother. "Yes," Bill had replied. "I heard somebody but I didn't know who it was."

William paused and the Court was silent as everyone waited for him to resume. "It seems very hard to tell upon my own brother," he sighed before continuing. " He put his hand upon my arm and he said, 'I've been and killed two Policemen!' That's what he said to me. I didn't know what to do with myself. I was frightened nearly to death." Henry had then told him that he had lost his hat in the affray and he had remarked to his brother that he would not find it, as it was too dark. Both Henry and Frank had run off along the road. Shortly after, Day had caught up with him and they had walked back home. They had then come across a body, which he thought was one of the Policemen. "We stopped about two or three minutes and looked at it. Day said, 'I can't hear him breathe.' I said,'No more can't I. It might be somebody drunk."

The two men had stood there for a while until Tidbury had said; 'Come on Bill.' and the two men had walked on. "I did tremble. I could not help it when my brothers told me they had killed two Policemen." Day and he had gone home and gone to bed. He had gone to work the next morning and had been detained there by Superintendent Bennett. "I told Mr Bennett a lie. I did it to favour my brother as much as I could but I knowed it would be no good. I told him I was in bed at half past eight the night the murder was done. Mr Bennett told me that he had my two brothers and William Day. I told him I could not help it and I was innocent... I was not there when the murder was done." Tidbury sat down and the formal proceedings at the Magistrates' Court concluded with the four men being committed to the Berkshire Assizes.

Between the committal proceedings and the Assizes the Police conducted yet another search and their diligence was rewarded when one of the missing gun barrels was found along the banks of the millstream near the cottages. Another gun barrel was discovered between the houses lived in by the various members of the families.

PART TWO

The trial of the prisoners commenced at Reading in February 1877. They were all charged with the murder of P.C.Shorter and such was the interest that admission was by ticket only.

The accused shuffled into the dock and stood before the Judge, Mr Justice Lindley. In an age riddled with class distinction, where everyone 'knew his place', the four countrymen who were obviously from the bottom end of the scale must have felt completely out of touch with reality as barristers in wigs and gowns with 'upper class' accents sauntered in and out of the Court carrying books heavy with law. As the Judge took his place on the bench, bewigged and carrying a nosegay, and scrutinised them with the full majesty of the law behind him, surely they must have been aware that they were in a different world to the one they usually inhabited at Hungerford. Yet here they were on trial for their lives, within an ace of meeting the hangman. Each one of them must have felt his position keenly.

The Clerk of the Assize, now facing the prisoners, called out their names and as he did so each man touched his forehead with his right index finger in acknowledgement. The charge of murdering P.C. Shorter was put to them and they all pleaded 'Not guilty.'

The barristers engaged in the case sat in front of them; Mr J.O. Griffiths Q/C for the prosecution, Mr Baker-Smith for Henry and Francis Tidbury and Mr Montague Williams for William Tidbury and William Day.

After outlining the case the first witnesses were called; P.C. Isaacs, who had met the Inspector, John Green, who had seen P.C. Shorter making his way towards his 'point' with his Inspector and, unknowingly, his fatal encounter with the murderers. Then P.C. Golby described to the Court finding the bodies of the Policemen and his actions of that December night. Cross-examined by Mr Baker - Smith he insisted that it was not consistent with the appearances of the deceased officers that they had been the instigators of the affray that had resulted in their deaths, as their staves (truncheons) had not been drawn. Shorter, he pointed out, had been in possession of a night-stick in addition to his undrawn truncheon whilst Drewitt had only a light cane. He had to admit that at first, when he had come across the body of P.C. Shorter, he had thought that it was a drunken man lying in the road.

A Mr Franklin then said that he had found P.C. Shorter's night-stick with blood and hair on it, in a field near the tollgate close to a gap in the hedge.

P.C. Brown, the Kintbury Constable, who had assisted Golby in the search for their Inspector, added something which virtually condemned one of the accused. After the prisoners had been arrested and taken before the magistrates, he had been in a room with Harry Tidbury who had suddenly muttered, "Mr Brown, I never blamed you for anything." P.C. Brown had answered, "I do not think that you did Harry."

Harry then made a damning admission. "That cap that you've got is mine. I was there and I am a guilty man!" Taken aback by this all that the Constable could say was that he had better prepare for his maker. "I've been trying to do so," was the pathetic rejoinder.

A shoemaker, William Williams, who had assisted the Police in the removal of Drewitt's body, stated that he had seen Day in a public house with a tobacco box like the one found near the corpse. In fact, on the day before the murders, when he had asked for some tobacco, Day had brought the box out, had broken off a twist and had given it to him. When questioned about this by Montague Williams however, he had to concede that he had never actually seen Day smoke or chew tobacco and, when he looked at it more closely, he admitted that it was after all a very ordinary tobacco box.

Dr. Major repeated his evidence, given at the inquest, of the injuries inflicted on the two Policemen.

William Hedges, the toll keeper, acknowledged that when he had seen Day and Bill Tidbury on the night of December 11th neither of them had been in possession of a gun.

Amos Batt, the next witness, had been at the tollgate earlier that night, about 7pm when he had seen the Tidburys and heard Day call out, "Bill!" behind them. Batt had, in the early hours of the following morning, assisted P.C. Brown in removing Inspector Drewitt's body and had seen Harry Tidbury's cap which had been concealed underneath. It was the same cap that he had seen Harry wearing just a few hours earlier near the tollgate.

Superintendent Bennett strode into the witness box. He told of the finding of the tobacco box, the trigger plate near the Inspector's body, the boot marks near the scene of the murders, of which he had taken wax impressions and the arrests of the four accused. The boots of Henry Tidbury, he maintained, corresponded with the impressions he had obtained, as did those of Frank Tidbury. He also produced the clothing worn by the prisoners at the time of their arrests. He was of the opinion that bloodstains were on all of the items shown; leggings, breeches, hats and trousers and he had submitted them for scientific examination. Whilst searching Day's cottage he had found the gun, which he produced, standing in the corner with an exploded cap on the nipple. The muzzle was black and it seemed to have been recently fired. When Bennett mentioned that the gun matched the indentations in Shorter's helmet, Mr Justice Lindley drily commented that it might be the case with any gun.

The Superintendent had also seized a bag containing mixed shot and another holding gunpowder as well as a powder flask.

On 18th December, whilst engaged in a search of the garden at the rear of the houses, he had chanced upon a broken gun stock in a couch heap and another stock by some ivy. The trigger plate discovered near Drewitt's body fitted this stock.

Later, he had dug up a gun barrel buried about 10 or 12 feet from the place where the first stock had been found. There were bloodstains on this stock as well and it gave the appearance of having recently been broken.

Mr Baker-Smith rose to cross-examine. "Could not the footprints have been made a month before?"

"Having regard to the heavy rain that night, no!" was the emphatic retort.

Superintendent Wiltshire said that he had been present when the stains on the clothing had been pointed out to Day. The prisoner had replied that they had been caused when he had caught some rabbits.The next witness, Sergeant Bull, had searched the cottage where Frank Tidbury lived with his mother and father and had come across the axe handle with fresh blood on it.

Dr. Tidey of the London Hospital had examined the clothing of the accused. He had, he related, found bloodstains on the clothing of Bill and Frank Tidbury and also Day but none on that belonging to Henry Tidbury. Nor were there any on Day's or Bill Tidbury's boots. Dr. Tidey went into great detail for the benefit of the Court of his findings and their position on the clothing and the fact that they were not old. He had to accept that although the stains were mammalian in origin he was unable to state categorically that they were human. There were red lead marks, he said, on some of the clothing.

The prosecution now brought forward a local hairdresser, Samuel Hanks, who alleged that shortly before the murders had occurred Harry Tidbury had called at his barber's shop. They had been discussing the recent murder of the Somerset Policeman when Hanks had asked what Harry would do if a gamekeeper caught him in the act of taking pheasants. "Shoot the bugger! Or rip him up sooner than be took" had been the unequivocal reply, before adding that if it was a Policeman or anyone else he knew he would not kill them but would"... bloody well punish them before they should have me." This conversation had been overheard by a journeyman printer and he now corroborated it.

Another witness was also produced to say that he had heard Day threaten that he would 'smash' anyone who attempted to take him. (Day had murmured that he would do well to remember the Commandment, "Thou shalt not bear false witness", when this evidence had been given at the lower Court.)

Sergeant Butcher now stepped into the witness box and said that he had been in charge of the accused when they had been conveyed by railway to the various Police Stations whilst they had been on remand. Day had remarked to the other prisoners, "Well, come Tuesday I shall speak up for myself. I am innocent. You know you three done it. What did you want to leave me at the farm for? And when you came down the road what did you want to tell me that the man lay in the road drunk for, when you knew what it was all the while and that you done it? Didn't you come in, in the morning and say if anyone asks me if I knowed anything about the man as lay in the road last night, I was to know nothing about it? You know you did and if you speaks the truth you can't deny it. If I'm hung it'll be through you three and you know it. I didn't know you had my gun out. I know nothing about how that cap came on the nipple."

The others had made no response to this incriminating statement, the Sergeant added, although it had been said loud enough for them all to hear. Later, on the same train between Newbury and Reading, he had reminded William and Frank Tidbury of what Day had said. "Bill Day's making it rather warm for you," he had remarked. William Tidbury looked the Sergeant straight in the eyes and replied enigmatically, "You don't know so much about Day as I do."

This concluded the evidence for the Prosecution and there being no witnesses for the defence and the prisoners being unable to give evidence on their own behalf [8], Mr Griffiths, for the Crown, now addressed the jury. He emphasised that when Day and William Tidbury had been seen at the toll-gate, the toll keeper had been asked if he had seen them in possession of guns and he had answered that he had not. If they were guilty they would not have carried them openly but have them disjointed in their pockets. Mr Griffiths pointed out that several witnesses had heard the firing of guns and it would have been at the time that the prisoners had encountered the two Police Officers. The footprints found later matched the boots

---

8 *Accused persons were not allowed to give evidence on their behalf at Quarter Sessions or Assizes until the passing of the Criminal Evidence Act, 1898.*

worn by the prisoners and the tobacco box chanced upon at the scene was said to belong to Day along with the cord which he used for ferreting. The gun which had been retrieved from his cottage fitted the marks on P.C. Shorter's helmet. Henry Tidbury's cap had been found by the body of the Inspector and he had admitted to P.C. Brown when he was in custody that it belonged to him. William Tidbury had lied to Superintendent Bennett, when he had been arrested, about being at home, when he had been seen by the Hedges and Frank Tidbury's boot marks had been clearly proved to have been made that night. Finally, Mr Griffiths commented, though the two murdered Police Officers had been powerfully built men their lives had been taken with great violence and although the prisoners did not appear to be able to overpower them, collectively they were capable of doing just that.

Mr Baker-Smith, counsel for Henry and Frank Tidbury, rose and reminded the jury that his clients were employed in regular work and all the witnesses had said that they were of quiet and peaceful dispositions. There was no motive for the killings; plunder was not the object nor were there any grounds for revenge against the Policemen. He then asked the jury if the subsequent behaviour of his clients were the actions of guilty men. They had not, as criminals, taken flight but had gone to work. Mr Baker-Smith next dismissed the statement made by Day in the railway carriage as being misheard by the Sergeant owing to the noise of the train and he queried why the prudent silence of the others should give rise to an adverse inference against them. Whilst he allowed that the case against Henry Tidbury might be one of manslaughter, the evidence produced against Frank Tidbury was, at least, such as to justify his acquittal.

Mr Montague Williams for the other two prisoners disposed of the case against them by firstly observing that neither man had been shown to have a gun, yet the theory was that his clients and the two other prisoners had started off in a pre-arranged scheme of night poaching at a particular spot. Yet William Day and William Tidbury had actually gone to work on an engine nearby, in the very locality where, the prosecution alluded, they had intended to commit the highly penal offence of night poaching. "How improbable!" he expostulated. "But this improbability was surpassed by others." The Superintendent had told the Court that the blow inflicted on P.C. Shorter's helmet was from Day's gun and such was the force that it had penetrated the metal band. Yet the lock on Day's gun was quite undamaged and there was no blood or marks on it when it had been found standing, quite openly, in the room of his house when he had been arrested. To say that the marks upon Shorter's helmet had been made by this gun were a little less than absurd. The other guns had been hidden and they were broken and the lock of one had been entirely shattered. Counsel impressed on the jury that Day had not told one lie throughout the proceedings right from the time he had been detained. "And where was Day when he had been taken into custody?" he demanded of the twelve good men sitting opposite him. "Why, quietly having breakfast." Montague Williams paused to let the importance of that sink in before continuing, "What did he say at the moment of apprehension, a most critical time ? The truth and it had been corroborated. He had described his proceedings at the farm, which was borne out by witnesses and had stated that William Tidbury had left before him. Both he and Tidbury had walked calmly past the toll keeper and his wife, entering into conversation with them about them shivering, which was the truth again," he reminded the jury, "for he had been standing about doing work on the engine at the farm."

He had then told of returning from the farm and the course he took would have been one where he could not have seen the body of the Inspector in the lane. He had admitted seeing the corpse of P.C. Shorter and that he believed what he had been told by his companion that night, that it was a drunken man. Montague Williams then reminded the jury that P.C. Golby, when he had first encountered his colleague's body, had thought it was a drunk lying in the road and had pushed it with his stick. It had not been until he had lit his lamp that he had realised that it was a dead body.

Counsel now referred to the statement Day had made in the train when he had been on remand. He felt that he was being dragged into the crime and it was natural that, in an instinct of self-preservation, he should have said what he did.

Going on to the tobacco box found at the scene and on which the authorities had placed so much reliance, said Montague Williams, these were sold by the thousands at country fairs and if it was Day's it was most likely to have been borrowed by one of the Tidburys who, being related, could and did enter Day's room and avail themselves of such a trifle.

Defence Counsel now described the shot found in Day's pouch as 'not unusual' and as to the gun, the Tidburys had the opportunity of using that as well.

He came now to the blood on Day's jacket and asked the jury, "Where do ferreters who carry rabbits sling them when they are dead and bleeding? Why, over their left shoulder. Even the able and qualified London doctor who examined the blood could not say it was recent."

Finally, after he had exhorted the jury to bring in a true and exonerating verdict, Mr Montague Williams sat down.

Mr Justice Lindley now began his summing up and informed the jury as to the law relating to the culpability of those persons engaged in unlawful acts and who, in order to evade capture or detection, killed a Policeman or were present when such an act was committed. Then he went on to sift through the evidence that had been given in Court. Nothing was known of the activities of the other prisoners when they had been seen in the company of William Tidbury passing up the Wantage Road, though it had been suggested that they were in the wood shooting. With regard to the footprints that had been found, the Judge was not convinced that they had those peculiar marks which were similar to those boots worn by Day and would lead the jury to say that they positively were his. They were like his, he conceded, but the jury must be satisfied that the fourth set of footprints found were Day's and had been made at the same time as the others, because the jury must not lose sight of the fact that he was employed at the farm and would presumably travel that route often to and from his place of employment. He left it to them to decide if they were Day's and were made contemporaneously with the others.

Mr Justice Lindley examined the finding of the ferret line and the tobacco box and reminded the jury that they had to be certain when Day had dropped them. Then he referred to the guns found and whether any of them fitted the indentations on Shorter's helmet. He advised them to take these exhibits and to see which of them fitted with any accuracy and to make their own inference. Assuming that Day's gun was out that night, had he got it? There was no direct evidence whatever and as to the shot, supposing, asked the Judge that it had come out of Day's bag, had he used it that night?

Mr Justice Lindley then discussed the evidence against the other accused. He pointed out that Henry Tidbury's footprints had been identified by several witnesses and his cap had been found under the body of the Police Inspector and he had made an incriminating statement about it.

Turning to William Tidbury he said that no blood had been found on his clothing. He had shivered as he passed the tollgate although that might be fairly attributable to the cold. He had also made a statement before the magistrates and the Judge asked the jurors to be aware of the fact that there was $^3/_4$ hour not accounted for. He asked them to bear in mind, taking all the facts in consideration, whether William Tidbury was with the others and that the footprints were his.

He now came to the last prisoner, Frank Tidbury. He recalled that his boots were very erratically nailed and these peculiar prints had been found near the picket fence and also in the cow dung. He had said nothing when he had been apprehended and when the statements had been made by his co-accused before the magistrates and in the train he had said nothing nor offered any contradiction. The jury must consider the sufficiency of the evidence against him as against all the prisoners. After giving them instruction on the difference in law between murder and manslaughter, the judge left the members of the jury to consider their verdict.[9]

After deliberating for two hours they returned and the entire Court waited in anticipation for the outcome. William Day they acquitted; William Tidbury, they decided, was guilty of being an accessory after the fact of murder; Henry Tidbury they found guilty of murder as they did his brother Francis, although they added a recommendation of mercy on account of his age and that in their opinion,"this deplorable murder was an unpremeditated one."

Mr Justice Lindley observed that as William Tidbury had not been indicted for being an accessory he could not therefore be found guilty on that matter. With that, both he and Day were removed from the dock. The Judge now turned his attention to the two remaining prisoners. "Henry and Francis George Tidbury, you have been found guilty after a long, patient and careful enquiry of the murder of Police Constable Shorter on the night of 11th December last and although it will be my duty to forward to the proper authorities the recommendation of the jury with respect to you, Francis George Tidbury, it is my duty and I have no option but to discharge that duty to pass sentence of death upon both of you. It will rest, not with me but with those who are entrusted by law with greater responsibilities than even mine to determine what effect, if any, will be given to that recommendation. All I can say is I shall take care to transmit it to the proper quarter. But that the verdict is warranted by the evidence is a matter upon which I do not think there can be much, if any, difference of opinion. I shall not enlarge upon it....I must say that although the case has been established against you by circumstantial evidence and by that alone, it warranted the conclusion come to. It is, to say the least of it, most creditable that through the diligence shown by the Police Officers, Golby and Superintendent Bennett, this matter has

9 *It had been a two day trial. At the end of the first day the jury had been taken to The Queens Hotel in Reading where they stayed overnight in one large room with fourteen beds provided.*

been brought to light. It is not, happily for us, the law that no crime can beproved by circumstantial evidence, that is not the law here nor, so far as I know, in any civilised society. But if that were the law there would be no safety on the part of anybody, for it would come to this, that there could be no conviction of anyone charged with murder unless the crime was perpetrated in the presence of a witness. I shall make no further comment but pass sentence." After he had sentenced the two men to be hanged they were taken away and the Court adjourned.

When it re-convened, William Day and William Tidbury were both brought up on the second indictment for the murder of Inspector Drewitt. However the Prosecution offered no evidence and a formal verdict of 'Not guilty ' was entered and the two men were released.

Whilst they were in Reading Gaol awaiting their fate, Henry and Frank sent letters to their mother, details of which were published in the press. They both wrote that the two other men had not taken any part in the murders..."Rest yourselves contented about my poor brother William and Day for they were not there when it was done..." Henry wrote, whilst Frank, in his letter said"...very glad that Day got out of this trouble thank God...."

When their parents visited them they were interviewed by reporters from the press. Both sons had asked forgiveness from the widows of the two men they had killed, they said.

A rather curious letter was published in one of the local papers in which the foreman of the jury explained why Day and William Tidbury had been acquitted. Apparently in the deliberations the jury had considered the case made out against these two men that they had been seen to go through the toll-gate immediately after the murders without a gun in their hands, the inference being that it had been secreted in the pockets of their jackets. What they, the jury, had considered was that if the gun had been broken and so placed, the exploded cap would have fallen off the nipple when the hammer had been raised to allow it to have been placed in their pockets. An exploded cap, not fitting tight like an unexploded one,..."as anyone acquainted with guns well knows." It had been clear, in the minds of the jury, that if Day and William Tidbury had passed by the toll gate immediately after the murders had taken place without guns being seen in their hands and also not in their pockets, the gun found in Day's house could not have been in the possession of either men minutes after the crime had been committed. "Viewed from this light," the letter went on" the prosecution against these two men falls to the ground."

When there was no response to the jury's recommendation that mercy should be shown to Frank Tidbury a petition was sent to the Home Office; according to one newspaper it was over fourteen yards in length. The Home Secretary replied that there were no grounds for a reprieve. At least one person was so irate at this reply that he wrote a letter to the Daily News, taking the Home Secretary to task for inconsistency. He referred to the recent murder of a Policeman at Manchester. A youth named Habron had been convicted and the jury had added the same recommendation for mercy on account of his youthfulness and his sentence had been commuted to Penal Servitude for life. The point the writer was trying to make was that Frank Tidbury was younger than Habron and the correspondent wanted to know on what grounds one man was reprieved whilst another was hanged. The Home Secretary was unmoved.[10]

A further letter written by Henry Tidbury was now published wherein he alleged that during the fight between the Police and the brothers the gun had gone off, accidentally wounding the Inspector.

The law took its inevitable course and on Monday, 12th March at 8am both men were executed by Marwood. It was apparently the first hanging at Reading Gaol since public executions had been abolished.

As soon as they had been hanged the newspapers rushed into print the confessions that had been penned by the doomed men in their last

10 The Habron brothers were charged with the murder of P.C. Cock of the Lancashire Constabulary. William Habron was the only one found guilty and was sentenced to death, although a recommendation of mercy was forwarded to the Home Secretary on account of his youthfulness. On this occasion he agreed and the sentence was commuted to Penal Servitude for life. Two years later, that notorious Victorian murderer and burglar, Charles Peace, admitted that he and not Habron had slain the Constable. William Habron was released and was given £800. The presiding Judge at the trial of the Habrons had been Mr Justice Lindley.

remaining days. Henry admitted that they had gone poaching that night in December and that they were on their way home when the two Police Officers had accosted them and they, the poachers, had run off. "... The Police caught hold of Frank and I went back to them." he had written. "Then they caught hold of me and we had a struggle. They said,'Tidbury is that you?' And I found that we could not get away. Then I shot him and he fell down. The other Policeman caught hold of us. He found that we were too much for him and he run away and my brother and me run after him and we hit him with our guns when he was down and killed him then. We went back and Mr Drewitt was staggering in the road and I hit him again but I don't know whether my brother hit him or not. Mr Drewitt said,'Don't kill a man.' But we took no notice for we were excited at it."

Recounting their meeting with their brother William and telling him that they had just killed the Policeman, Henry added "..I don't think my brother would begin rough with them if I had not begun first. After I began I told Francis to hit them and Francis began with them and shot his gun towards Shorter. Then Shorter ran away and we both run after him." Frank's confession corroborated his brother's. After their initial encounter with the Police when they had been surprised by them he went on;"We were all struggling together, then Henry's gun went off, I don't know whether he pulled the trigger or not, I can't say. Mr Drewitt fell down and Mr Shorter ran away and Henry ran down after him and I ran after Henry. When I got to him he had knocked Shorter down and then I hit him a time or two. I can't say how often I hit him. I hit him on the head with the barrel of my gun, the one which was not broken. Then we went to Mr Drewitt. Then we hit him."

An additional statement made by Francis was published in which he said that when the Policemen had arrived he had put his gun down by the pheasants he had just shot. The Police had heard Henry's gun being fired. Telling P.C. Shorter that they had nothing, the Constable had replied that it did not matter; he (Francis) was to go along with him. He had picked up his gun and had shot at the Constable and he had run off. Both he and his brother had pursued Shorter and had beaten him to death when they had caught up with him. He had seen the dead Constable's helmet lying in the road and he had picked it up and had thrown it over the hedge. Frank continued, "After having killed Shorter we went to Mr Drewitt who was not dead and I hit him on the head and other places. Just before we got to him Drewitt said,'Oh don't kill a fellow!' Then after we had killed him we went away and met my brother William who came to us and we all three went back to Mr Drewitt to see if we could find Henry's hat. Then William struck a light. We could not see the hat. Then he told us to go home. While we were going across Folly field I said I saw a light where Mr Shorter was. I suppose that was the other Policeman."

For his actions on that dreadful winter's night P.C. Golby was promoted to Sergeant and a subscription was raised by the local magistrates for a presentation to Superintendent Bennett.

Two crosses mark the places where the two Policemen met their fate and they now lie at rest in the nearby churchyard.

The poaching war in this country is a long and bloody one stretching back into the far distant past and continuing up to the present time. Several Policemen and gamekeepers have been killed by men intent upon taking game illegally. Once, poaching might have been done out of necessity. Now it is committed out of sheer greed. Whatever the reason, nothing can alter the fact that in Berkshire in the 1870s four men were killed for the sake of a brace of pheasants.

Roadside memorial to P.C. Shorter at the scene of his murder.

Roadside memorial to Inspector Drewitt at the scene of his murder.

'In death they were not divided'. The graves of Inspector Drewitt and P.C. Shorter.

"A DISGRACEFUL STATE OF AFFAIRS..."

POLICE CONSTABLE JOHN JOSEPH CHARLTON
Berkshire Constabulary - 1899

For twenty-three years after the atrocious murders of Inspector Drewitt and P.C. Shorter, the officers of the Berkshire Constabulary went about their business in the quiet way that had become expected of the British Police. A typical officer was Police Constable John Joseph Charlton who had in his career served at various places within the county; Maidenhead, Twyford, Abingdon and now at East Hendred where he had been the village constable for twelve years. He had suffered personal tragedy, when in 1894 his eldest boy had been run over and killed by a wagon. He was one of those sterling members of the Constabulary who carried on his work with little thought of advancement and in his own unspectacular fashion. On Easter Monday, April 3rd 1899, he was assisting his colleague, Thomas Hewitt, who was the constable for the nearby village of Harwell.

By 8pm things were becoming a little too boisterous for Isaac Day, the landlord of the Chequers Inn at Harwell. The majority of his customers had been drinking for the best part of the day and were by now somewhat noisy. This was now topped by one of them, Joseph Slatter, not only beginning to sing but then passing his hat around the clientele of the public house, in effect begging for money. This was the last straw for Day and he ordered Slatter to leave the premises. When the drunken reveller refused to quit, P.C. Hewitt was called for and he was asked by the exasperated landlord to eject Slatter and his friend Robert James who, in his own drunken way, wanted to help his chum.

It was never going to be easy and ultimately P.C. Charlton was called upon to assist his comrade.

P.C. John Joseph Charlton. (Berkshire Constabulary)

The Chequers Public House, Harwell, about the time that P.C. Charlton was killed.

The Chequers Public House at Harwell,.

As the men struggled in the taproom, P.C. Hewitt was assaulted by both the men he was trying to eject, but eventually the two Constables with the assistance of Day managed to put the recalcitrant men outside the public house.

Both the Constables, showing great restraint under the circumstances, advised Slatter and James to leave as quietly as possible but, as so often happens in public house brawls, the two offenders could not leave well enough alone. Slatter called out, "Now Bob, give it to the buggers! Knife them! I will back you." The assault on the Constables was renewed with a ferocious intensity.

Slatter immediately hit Hewitt whilst James started on the other Policeman. Hewitt fell to the ground but noticed that Charlton was faring even worse than he was, for James had kicked him, in consequence of which Charlton had fallen on his back, striking his head and becoming unconscious.

Whilst on the ground both Constables were kicked repeatedly. Eventually, after several minutes struggling, P.C. Hewitt managed to get to his feet and subdued James and Slatter, handcuffing the latter, whilst the former, deciding that discretion was now the better part of valour, quit the field of battle and made off.

P.C. Charlton meanwhile was removed to the Police house in Harwell and the local doctor, Dr. Rice, was summoned to attend him. There was little he could do and at 8pm the next day P.C. Charlton succumbed to his injuries. P.C.Hewitt had emerged from the fracas with a fractured nose and with both eyes blackened. During the course of the struggle he had had to send someone for his truncheon and handcuffs before he was able to restrain his prisoner.[1]

A post-mortem was performed on the body of Charlton[2] and Dr. Rice discovered that the cause of death was a fracture to the base of the skull, which in his opinion was caused either when he fell to the ground striking his head or by one of the kicks that had been inflicted on the constable whilst he was on the ground.

1 Although several witnesses stated that both Police Officers were sent for, one testified that they were already in The Chequers in plain clothes whilst another, which might give that some credence, alleged that Slatter and James had called out, "Come out and fight you tecs detectives)!" This might explain why Hewitt had to send someone to his house for his truncheon and handcuffs, although sometimes a Polices Officer did not carry these accoutrements as a matter of course. 2 I can find no reference as to where the actual post mortem took place, surely not at the Police house! It had been long known for them to be performed at public houses in the earlier part of the nineteenth century.

'In custody' Slatter and James.

The search was now on for James and he was arrested two days later by P.C. Tibbs of the Oxfordshire Constabulary whilst in a public house at Stoke Row.

The Inquest was held[3] and several witnesses testified as to the violence of the attack upon the two constables, whilst adding that the Police had behaved at all times quite properly towards the prisoners. Most of the crowd had taken no part in the fray and had stood by idly and watched. A fact commented on by a local paper.[4]

The Coroner's jury, after a short deliberation, returned a verdict of wilful murder[5], complimenting P.C. Hewitt on his conduct. The Coroner, echoing the stance of the Reading Mercury, commented sourly, "Here were men discharging their duty and yet the crowd of twenty to thirty stood there in indifference whilst the Constables were set upon by two roughs. It is a disgraceful state of affairs."

The two prisoners were now committed for trial by the Wantage Magistrates and such was the depth of revulsion felt against them

---

3 Through to the early part of the twentieth century, inquests in country districts were held usually at village inns, these being the focal point of the community. 4 The Reading Mercury. 5 Until the mid-twentieth century a Coroner's jury could give a verdict of 'wilful murder' and commit to Azzizes.

that it was thought necessary to provide twenty Policemen as escort to ensure their safety.

At the Berkshire Summer Assizes, the Bill of Indictment for murder when laid before the Grand Jury was rejected on the advice of the Judge and the charge was reduced to that of Manslaughter.[6]

The evidence was proceeded with and the two prisoners testified from the witness box that both they and the Police Officers were drunk.[7]

The (petit) jury spent little time considering what their verdict would be. Both men were guilty of the Manslaughter of P.C. Charlton.

The Judge, in passing sentence, told the prisoners that he considered it a very bad case of manslaughter, gross and hideous in fact, and that the lives of the Police should be respected by those who had to administer the law, if not by ruffians such as the prisoners, and their lives would be avenged on those who took them. He added that both the slain Officer and his colleague had behaved admirably throughout the encounter and that in justice to the Police and for the protection of society the sentence of the Court would be that each man would serve twenty years penal servitude.[8]

The Chequers Public House, Harwell. (As it is today)

6 Grand Juries were abolished in the 1930s in England. 7 Prisoners being allowed to give evidence on their own behalf had been introduced under the Criminal Evidence Act 1898. 8 Both prisoners were thoroughly bad lots. Slatter, also known as Abingdon Jack, had joined the Royal Marines in 1879 but had had to leave. He had thirty previous convictions before the Harwell affray. James had been in The East Kent Regiment and had apparently been a champion boxer. Since leaving the Army he had several offences recorded against him, including a recent appearance before Wantage Magistrates for poaching.

"...CONTINUED ON THEIR MERRY WAY."

INSPECTOR FRANCIS JOHN EAST
Berkshire Constabulary - 1944

During the Second World War Britain became host to men of many different nationalities who made their way to this country in a determination to pursue the struggle against the common foe, Nazi Germany. This was especially so after the fall of France in 1940 and also on a vastly increased scale when the United States entered the conflict in 1941 and sent her vast armies of men to these islands, not only to maintain an aerial bombardment against the enemy, but also to prepare with the allies for the eventual invasion of occupied Europe.

For propaganda purposes during these hard and dangerous times, it was expedient to show to the world that the ordinary men and women of the allies were getting on famously together. As a generalisation this was correct, but it was not always strictly true and some persons of the host nation resented those who had come to these shores. Unfortunately this animosity sometimes boiled over into more aggressive action and brawls would occur involving the service personnel of one country and those of another. These were, after all, men who were trained to be 'combat ready' and were therefore in a heightened state of preparedness for the greater battle which lay ahead. They were, no doubt, wound up as tight as any coiled spring and ever ready to vent their frustrations if pushed too far. Sometimes the animosity between the host nation and their 'guests' also resulted in arguments and fights. More often than not it was the Police, usually civilian, sometimes military, who had to sort matters out between the warring factions.

To a certain extent the brunt of these attacks, either verbal or physical, was directed against the Americans who, presumably because of their better pay and conditions and what was perceived to

Inspector Francis East. (Berkshire Constabulary)

be their free and easy attitude, especially it was thought towards British women, were resented most of all. At best they could be considered somewhat brash, at worst arrogant and the unfortunate expression " Over paid, over sexed and over here" was sometimes used in a vindictive way against American servicemen.

It was as a direct result of such a confrontation between civilians and members of the U.S.Army that Inspector Francis John East lost his life one autumn night in 1944.

On the evening of Wednesday, 4th October of that year Captain Joseph McKee of the United States Army had been driven from an Army camp in Oxfordshire to Maidenhead and he had arranged with the two soldiers who accompanied him, Private Joseph Frank Phillips and Private Estle James Styles, to collect him from the Riviera Hotel at 11 o'clock. The two privates, after dropping their Captain off, parked the Army truck in Bridge Road and went into town. Entering a public house they consumed three pints of beer. Leaving that establishment they went to another public house and purchased two-quart bottles of beer which they took back to their vehicle. Driving back into town they came across the Cresset Cafe in the High Street and, seeing that it was open, stopped their truck and decided that they would buy some sandwiches. Styles started to get out of the Army vehicle to go to the cafe whilst Phillips commenced talking to a girl who knew him by his nickname, 'Red'.

Whether the two civilians who then approached the Americans were aggrieved by seeing them apparently 'chatting up' a local girl or whether they just wanted to cause trouble is not known, but as they passed they made some remark about wanting to fight the American soldiers. Styles replied that he had no wish to fight but one of the civilians argued with him and put up his fists. Styles, naturally enough, sought to defend himself and a struggle ensued. Phillips likewise became engaged with the other civilian.

It was at this stage of the proceedings that Inspector East arrived on the scene and separated the combatants. He asked the two American servicemen what exactly had happened and they explained the circumstances to the Police Officer.

Inspector East took their names and recorded them in his notebook. Styles also mentioned that he and Phillips were on their way to pick up their Captain from the Riviera Hotel. Phillips, having given his details to the Policeman, may have believed that the incident was now closed or it is possible that that he thought it more prudent to leave before any further action took place. Whatever passed through his mind he now started up the truck and commenced driving it away.

Inspector East, however, had not yet finished with the Americans and jumped up onto the running board and grabbed hold of Styles who in turn pulled away from the Police Officer. East lost his grip and fell from the truck into the roadway.

The two Americans now made their way to the designated rendezvous but as they could not find their Captain returned to their base. On their way there Styles discovered that the Inspector's cap was in the truck and threw it out of the window.

Meanwhile Inspector East lay unconscious in the road at Castle Hill where he was found by a passer-by who contacted the Emergency Services. He was conveyed to Maidenhead Hospital where he was found to be suffering from multiple fractures of the skull, a broken jaw and arm and severe bruising. His injuries were so serious however that within fifteen minutes of admission to the hospital he died.

The Police quickly ascertained which U.S.Army base the truck involved in the fatal incident had come from and hurried there. They interviewed both Styles and Phillips. However, under an arrangement with the United States Authorities, the matter was now taken over and dealt with by their Military Police and their report into the matter was submitted directly to the Judge Advocate's Department.

In November, Privates Styles and Phillips appeared before a court-martial convened at Maidenhead Town Hall.

Castle Hill, Maidenhead, where Inspector East questioned the two Americans.
(As it is today)

Both men pleaded not guilty to the charges laid before them and the Military Court then heard the evidence of the witnesses. There was nothing contentious in their accounts leading up to where the Police Officer had intervened in the fracas, had separated the men and had commenced taking details. The truck was then driven off with the Inspector jumping up and eventually falling from it.

The two prisoners declined to give evidence on their own behalf but the Officer defending them submitted statements made by them earlier to the Court Martial. Styles, in his deposition, related that as he and Phillips drove off the Policeman had jumped onto the running board. He had told the Inspector that he had better get off as they had given him all the information he had requested and they had to leave. East had held on doggedly to Styles' forearm, almost pulling the serviceman out of the vehicle. He (Styles) had jerked back and immediately felt released from the Inspector's grip as he fell from the truck. He and Phillips had then gone looking for their Captain, had been unable to find him and had made their way back to their camp. Styles added that he had thrown the Inspector's cap out when he had seen it lying in the vehicle. He categorically denied striking East.

Phillips, in his statement, said that when he had given his particulars to Inspector East, Styles had said, "Let's go!" and he had started to drive the truck away. He had seen the Policeman on the running board pulling Styles. He had thought that East would jump from the truck and that was why he had not stopped.

Submitting that there was insufficient evidence to convict for manslaughter as there was nothing to say whether Inspector East had been pushed or had been thrown from the vehicle, the Defending Officer moved that the case against the two accused was not made out. He added that there was some evidence to show that East had sustained his most serious injuries when a passing taxi had run over him whilst he had been laying in the road after falling from the truck.

The Prosecuting Advocate argued that a man did not just step off a fast moving vehicle and added that when the Inspector was on the running board the accused Styles had either shaken him loose or pushed him off and it was reasonable to assume that when East fell he would injure himself. The accused had then, he said, "...continued on their merry way."

After a short recess both Styles and Phillips were found guilty and were sentenced to three years imprisonment with hard labour, to be dishonourably discharged from the Army and to forfeit all pay and allowances.

The forlorn grave of Inspector East.

"A CRIME OF UTTER RECKLESSNESS"

INSPECTOR JAMES BRADLEY
Oxfordshire Constabulary - 1966/67

For hundreds of years this country suffered from the depredations of roving bands of rogues and vagabonds who wandered far and wide, sometimes alone, but often in groups, committing any sort of criminal act, from poaching, thieving, burglary, robbery to even murder. Prior to the formation of the 'professional' Police in the nineteenth century these miscreants could only be harried by the local constable until they passed out of his parish or town and onto the next when it became the problem of that district's officials to sort out. Usually, unless it was that predator, the so called 'Gentleman of the road' the highwayman, these itinerants made their way about on foot and, if an offence was committed in one parish elsewhere, they could quite easily be traced, detained and dealt with under the harsh laws prevailing at the time.[1] Unless, however, the offence was a serious one it was doubtful if the parish that had suffered from these villains would sanction the expense of a pursuit.

The formation of the various county and borough Police forces throughout the country in the nineteenth century meant that offenders could now be hunted across parish, city and county boundaries.

With the advent of the railway system at more or less the same time, certain sections of the 'criminal classes' took advantage of this new mode of transport and travelled out from the cities that harboured them to commit their crimes, raiding country mansions and houses and returning to their dens or 'rookeries' to dispose of their plunder. 'Bill Sykes' had become mobile. Many a country Policeman was instructed to pay attention during the daylight hours to suspicious persons disembarking from trains at railway stations,[2] and it was not unknown for criminals to travel some distance to effect a raid on a

---

1 A good example of this is given in 'Murder in Buckinghamshire' by the author, of a roving band of two men and a women who killed the Western Turville toll-keeper and his wife in 1822. 2 This instruction was still in force in some Constabulary areas until recent times.

house if it was thought that it was worth their while and sometimes to use great violence in an effort to make good their escape. Thus, in 1885, some East End of London criminals travelled all the way to Cumberland, burgled the home of Sir Frederick Graham at Netherby Hall, were interrupted and, taking flight, shot and killed one Policeman[3] and wounded several others before being captured by astute Railwaymen.

The coming of the motor car in the early twentieth century proved another useful means of transport and the criminals took to this as easily as their predecessors had taken to the railways and Policemen everywhere now had to contend with a more mobile type of criminal - the so called 'Motor Bandit'.

Sometimes they could be just as dangerous as their criminal forbears, as in September 1927,when two hardened travelling gangsters, Frederick Guy Browne and William Henry Kennedy shot Police Constable George Gutteridge in a quiet country lane in the early hours of the morning when he stopped them in a car they had just stolen. Co-operation between Police Forces had also improved and criminals could not rely upon committing crime in one area, leaving it and escaping detection, especially where the crime was a heinous one such as murder, for Browne was eventually arrested in London whilst Kennedy was captured in Liverpool for the murder which had taken place in the Essex Police District.

In the early 1930s, Police Forces all over the country established Road Traffic Departments, the main aim being to police the ever increasing amount of vehicles on the roads. Another was to attempt to counter the incursions of these travelling criminals and to this end occasional roadblocks were set up in an effort to catch them.

In the days following the end of the Second World War, as people steadily became better off so more of the population took to the car. This was especially true of criminals who could now roam virtually at will throughout the length and breadth of the country, commit crime and vanish back into the cities almost without trace, using the

---

3 *P.C. Byrnes of the Cumberland and Westmoreland Constabulary.*

ever expanding system of motorways to facilitate their passage. The Police, especially those in more rural areas, had now more than ever to be on the alert for these villains, some of whom would literally stop at nothing to evade arrest.

Inspector James Bradley of the Oxfordshire Constabulary was to become the victim of one such incident in late 1966. James Bradley, known affectionately to his colleagues as 'Puffer', had joined the Police in 1946. Promoted to the rank of Inspector on 1st January, 1966, he had been posted to Banbury.

Inspector James Bradley. (Oxfordshire Constabulary)

It was the era of the so called 'Swinging Sixties',when just about anything went. Women's skirts went up, further than they had ever done before, and morals appeared to go down lower than they had ever done, at least arguably since the eighteenth century. Crime, to the amazement of those who had said that it was caused by poverty, soared in an age of affluence and high employment. It was the age of, 'You've never had it so good' and, over thirty years later we are still paying for it.

Meanwhile,as his forefathers had done before,the travelling criminal continued to ply his trade.

In late November 1966,Samuel Woodrow, a 20 year old plumber of Notting Hill, hired an Austin A60 Cambridge saloon motor car from a dealer in Kilburn Lane, Kensington, London. It was doubtful if he intended to use it just to drive about in, for although Woodrow was of previous unblemished character, his associate, George Edward Pugh, a 26 year old window cleaner, had several previous findings of guilt as a juvenile and convictions as an adult for housebreaking, larceny and burglary. He had also recently been charged by the Metropolitan Police for being a suspected person loitering with intent and was currently on bail to appear at Court.

Christmas was only a few weeks away and most people's thoughts were concentrated on buying cards and presents for loved ones and, in an effort to highlight the festivities, towns, cities and villages throughout the United Kingdom were putting up decorations.

On Saturday, 3rd December, a few days after he had hired the vehicle, Woodrow with his companion Pugh drove to the South Midlands town of Rugby. They were after the rich pickings they thought there were to be had from the 'good class dwelling houses', as they were described in Police parlance,that abound in certain parts of that town. They then intended to return to Notting Hill and dispose of or 'fence' their ill gotten gains. They sighted just such a house in Dunchurch Road, which the occupiers Mr and Mrs Bowden had left unoccupied earlier that day to visit Leicester. Pugh broke the glass in the front door of the house with his elbow, released the catch,opened the door and the two men entered the premises. It was shortly after at approximately 6.50pm that Mr and Mrs Bowden returned. They were somewhat disconcerted to see Woodrow and Pugh coming out of their drive, especially as one of them was carrying a case. The Bowdens next discovered that their house had been broken into and, suspecting that the two men they had just seen had something to do with it, followed them to where they had parked their car in a nearby service road. As it was driven off, Mrs Bowden bravely wrenched open the driver's door. She did not stop the two men from speeding off, but as the interior light came on she managed to obtain a good look at the two occupants. Mr Bowden, having taken the registration number of the car, now telephoned the Warwickshire Constabulary Headquarters, informing them that his house had been broken into, that property had been stolen and the criminals disturbed. He also gave the Police the number of the car in which they had made off and their direction of travel.

A message was hastily sent out to all Police cars in the vicinity and it was not long before P.C. Robert Livingstone of the Traffic Department with his observer, P.C. John Burrows patrolling in their car, call sign Charlie 4, spotted the vehicle and its occupants and began to closely follow it as the driver, Woodrow, tried to find his way back to London. At the same time, a Leamington patrol car, Alpha 3, manned by P.C.s Belcher and Murray were directed to Southam to conduct a road check. They placed their white patrol car in such a position that oncoming traffic could readily see the large reflective word 'Police' on the vehicle's side and with its blue light on the two officers waited apprehensively as they listened to the report of the pursuit over their car radio.

The fleeing criminals saw the stationary Police car as they approached it and Woodrow swung his car over to the left hand side of the road, onto the grass verge, past Alpha 3 and drove on. The two Constables, abandoning the road check, now joined in the chase behind Charlie 4.

It continued on along the Southam - Banbury road, through the darkness of the early evening, past Ladbroke and over the South Oxford canal at Fenny Compton,[4] the A.60 in front with the two Police cars, their blue lights gyrating and their two-tone horns blaring, following close behind.

Woodrow, in his mad flight through the Warwickshire and Oxfordshire countryside, caused several near accidents to other road users whilst Pugh threw some of the articles he and his mate had recently stolen out of the car window in a forlorn attempt to distract the drivers of the Police cars. This hare brained scheme failed as the experienced Police drivers resolutely shadowed their quarry whilst their colleagues, the 'observers', passed and received messages back to their Headquarters over their radios on the conduct of the chase.

When it could be seen that the Austin would not be stopped before it reached Banbury, Warwickshire Control Room contacted Oxfordshire Constabulary and informed them of the current position.

At Banbury it was thought that the only way to stop the headlong flight of the criminals' car was to set up a road block and accordingly Sergeant Harris and P.C. Patterson attempted to form one in the limited time they now had available. It was decided to lay on the block at the gates of the cemetery and with their Police van and two other vans they had commandeered, they started to set it up. Unfortunately there was a gap of several feet and, when a B.M.C. Mini-bus turned up, the driver was asked by the Police if they could use his vehicle to plug the space. He readily agreed but as he drove into a gateway, preparatory to placing his vehicle in the required position, it stalled and the driver could not restart it. The void was therefore not closed before the Austin Cambridge came into view closely followed by the two Warwickshire Police cars. Woodrow did not attempt to stop but drove straight at the two Police Officers manning the road block. Both jumped clear,one of them managing to throw his truncheon at the car in a vain attempt to smash the windscreen and thereby stop it.

4 *Where P.C. Hine of Warwickshire Constabulary had been murdered in 1886.*

Just before this had happened Inspector Bradley and Sergeant Hawkins had been walking along the road hurrying towards the road block. As it was being set up the Inspector shouted to his colleague, "Let's get down there!" and both men ran towards it to assist in whatever way they could. They could hear the sound of the two-tone horns coming ever nearer. As the two Police Officers watched the criminals' car go through the roadblock, Sergeant Hawkins stood in the road, signalling the driver to stop by raising his arm. Woodrow had no intention of complying and the Sergeant was forced to jump back onto the pavement to avoid being hit by the car. As he did so he noticed that the A60 swerved slightly and he could see his Inspector standing in the path of the careering vehicle, his arm extended holding a torch and waving it from side to side in a forlorn attempt to get the driver to halt. Woodrow did not and his car struck the Policeman, throwing him up into the air before he came back down onto the hard road surface. The A60 drove on at a speed of approximately 60mph.

Southam Road, Banbury, where Inspector Bradley was callously run down by fleeing burglars.

Another view of Southam Road, Banbury.

Still the criminals did not stop but carried on through the town, jumping a set of traffic lights set at red against them. The Leamington patrol car overtook both Charlie 4 and the A60 and forced Woodrow to swerve to his left. Woodrow then swung the car completely round and drove it back towards the traffic lights he had just crossed at high speed. P.C. Livingstone spun his patrol car round and followed the Austin through several narrow streets of Banbury and onto a dual carriageway. Woodrow,once more showing a complete disregard for others, drove his car onto the wrong side of the road before pulling over. P.C.s Livingstone and Burrows leapt from their car as they too stopped and quickly detained the two London villains. The pursuit at last was over! Woodrow stammered, "It was an accident! It was an accident!" before pleading pathetically with his captor,"Don't hit me!"

Both men were conveyed to Banbury Police Station where they were interviewed by Detective Inspector, (later Chief Inspector) Bill Boughton and Detective Superintendent Densham, head of the Oxfordshire C.l.D. Woodrow admitted driving the car, adding in a

The car which struck and fatally injured Inspector Bradley.

Another view of the car which struck Inspector Bradley.

statement he made later "..l drove all the time. I tried to make me(sic) way back to the M.1. I missed the turning...a Police car was driving behind me for a few miles, they wanted me to pull over and I thought,"Sod it! Let them give us a chase for a minute...".(we) went through the first road block and the second...there were two more officers, one moved out of the way and the other moved into me and there was nothing I could do about it."

When he was later charged with the attempted murder of the Police Inspector, Woodrow replied,"l will plead guilty to anything I am charged with."

Pugh, when interviewed admitted, riding with Woodrow and being concerned in the housebreaking in Rugby and telling Woodrow to "Go on!", when they were being pursued by the Police, as well as throwing articles from the car during the course of the chase. He further admitted shouting at Woodrow to keep going after he had knocked down Inspector Bradley. He then piously asked the interviewing detectives, "How is the Police Officer? I sincerely hope he gets better. I shall get life imprisonment, shan't I?"

The two men were placed in the cells and in an effort to get their story straight Pugh was overheard by a Police Officer to say to Woodrow,"It was an accident. You swerved to avoid him, got it?"

Meanwhile, Inspector Bradley, who had been taken to hospital, lingered on day by day, but despite all the ministrations and care of the staff he died of his injuries on New Years Day 1967. Woodrow and Pugh were now charged with his murder in addition to counts of housebreaking and dangerous driving.

When the two men appeared before Mr Justice Swannick at the Oxfordshire Assizes in March 1967 both men pleaded not guilty to murder; Woodrow also denied causing Inspector Bradley's death by reckless or dangerous driving and Pugh pleaded not guilty to aiding and abetting these offences. There were further offences put to Woodrow of dangerous driving in Warwickshire and the corresponding aiding and abetting offences for Pugh. These charges they also denied.

After legal submissions, the Judge instructed the jury that there was insufficient evidence to warrant a charge of murder against Pugh but that it was still open to them to find him guilty of manslaughter. The charge of murder was again put to Woodrow who pleaded not guilty but admitted manslaughter, as he did three cases of dangerous driving, which pleas were accepted by the Crown.

After hearing the case, Pugh's QC, Mr Edward Eveleigh, called no evidence on behalf of his client. The jury found Pugh guilty of the Inspector's manslaughter. Mr Justice Swannick addressed the men in the dock and commented, "This crime comes close to the borderline of murder. It was a crime of utter recklessness to escape from Justice and showed complete disregard for the lives of others. It culminated in the death of a Police Officer bravely doing his duty. The Police must be protected in their duty and lawlessness of this sort must be severely punished." The sort of severe punishment his Lordship had in mind was a sentence of eight years imprisonment for each man on the charge of manslaughter plus concurrent sentences on the other charges.[5]

5 *Compare these sentences with the twenty years penal servitude given to the two men convicted of the manslaughter of P.C. Charlton some sixty eight years earlier.*

"...THE ULTIMATE IN CRIMINALITY!"

DETECTIVE CONSTABLE IAN COWARD
Thames Valley Constabulary - 1971

PART ONE

In the 1960s there were a considerable number of Police mergers and reorganisations throughout the United Kingdom and a number of forces disappeared or were 'swallowed up' to form larger Police units. One of these amalgamations encompassed the five forces of Berkshire, Reading Borough, Buckinghamshire, Oxfordshire and Oxford City. The new force thus created on 1st April 1968 was to be henceforward known as the Thames Valley Constabulary. To cover this area there were over three thousand Policemen and women.

One of these Officers was Detective Constable Ian Coward. He had originally joined the Berkshire Constabulary as a cadet and then, in 1961, he had become a Constable. After being stationed at various places throughout that county, Ian transferred to the Traffic Department, met and married his wife, a junior shorthand typist at Sulhamstead House, which was then the headquarters of the Berkshire Constabulary and which is now the training school for the Thames Valley Police. In 1969 Ian moved to the Criminal Investigation Department based at Woodley near Reading. Two years on and his wife had given birth to a son, Matthew. The future for the Coward family seemed to be set fair.

There were others however, who did not have quite so pleasant a past, nor did they share a sense of responsibility towards their fellow man.

By 1971, Arthur William Skingle, aged 25, had been before the Courts on numerous occasions. At the age of 13 years he had a finding of guilt recorded against him for housebreaking. Over the

Detective Constable Ian Coward. (Thames Valley Constabulary)

course of the next two years he was sent first to an Approved School and then to Borstal. In 1964 he was sentenced to 21 months at the Old Bailey for armed robbery. He had escaped from prison twice and had then been arrested in 1967 for robbery. He had stayed the night at the flat of a man and the following morning he had stabbed his host in the back, tied and gagged him and stabbed him again before taking £100. He had been sentenced to seven years imprisonment. In April 1971 he had been transferred to the Pentonville pre-release hostel, a scheme whereby prisoners were allowed out of Prison to work but had to report back in the evenings. One June afternoon, after just a few weeks on the scheme, he failed to return to the hostel.

Peter George Sparrow, aged 28 years, had spent most of his childhood in care in local authority homes. At 15 he had been sent to an Approved School. At the age of 18 he had been sent for Borstal Training. In 1963 he was sent for another period of Borstal Training. Thereafter he served several prison sentences for theft and other offences.

In the late 1960s, for threatening three Police Officers with a sawn-off shotgun after breaking into a club at Eastbourne, he was sentenced to six years imprisonment, asking for 30 other offences to be taken into consideration. He had attempted to shoot at the pursuing Police during a high-speed chase but the cartridges in the shotgun he was using had failed to fire, otherwise the outcome might have been far more serious. Sparrow was, by 1971, also on the pre-release scheme at Pentonville but he too failed to return one evening. Both Sparrow and Skingle were now circulated as wanted and dangerous. Had either of them known it, they were destined to have only a few days of liberty. However, during the course of those days, they were both very active.

During the night of the 18th June, the armoury at the Whitgift School at Croydon was broken into and eight pistols, including an Astra make revolver, 700 rounds of ammunition, a 12 bore shotgun and cartridges were stolen by the abscondees now acting in concert with another criminal called Peter Cox. They were thus armed and extremely dangerous, especially to anyone who attempted to thwart them! Skingle and Sparrow then went to Brighton where, in the privacy of a hotel room, they set about shortening the barrels of the stolen shotgun. Shortly after, they stole a white Morris 1300 saloon car from a garage in Blackboys in East Sussex.

They then raided the manager's office of a petrol station at Little Warley in Essex in the middle of the night. The attendant was intimidated by one of the raiders, who thrust the barrel of a pistol into his stomach and was told, threateningly, "One peep out of you and that's it!" He was bound and gagged and £70 was stolen from the till. All these offences, to the detectives investigating them through the different Police Forces in southern England, were seemingly unconnected but all were to coalesce in a much more heinous crime at Reading towards the end of the month.

On the afternoon of Sunday, 27th June, whilst Reading was in the full throes of a 'Pop Festival', Sparrow was driving through the streets of the town accompanied by Skingle. Owing to their erratic driving they came to the notice of several other road users including the driver of a black Morris Traveller. This particular driver was Detective Constable Ian Coward and he was in an unmarked Police car. The occupants of the two cars were seen to be shouting at each other. D.C. Coward was informing Sparrow that he was a Police Officer and that he wanted him to pull over and stop. By the time both cars had reached Kings Road, the 1300 had come to a halt, its way ahead blocked by another car whilst D.C. Coward had positioned his Police car so that the driver of the 1300 could neither reverse nor drive off.

The detective got out of his car, walked up to Sparrow and once more informed him that he was a Police Officer, showing him his warrant card and intimating that he wanted to speak to him regarding his erratic driving. D.C. Coward asked for identification and Sparrow clambered out and, going to the boot of the car, went through the pretence of looking for something with which to identify himself. The detective walked back to the Police car, calling Sparrow over to him and telling him to sit in the passenger seat, whilst he resumed his position behind the steering wheel. The two villains with a stolen car and in possession of illegally held firearms must have been, by now, distinctly uneasy at this sudden turn of events

At Reading Police Station, busy with the Pop Concert, a call came through from Echo 12, Ian Coward's personal radio, requesting a check on an '1100' car registration number OOS 27G (the 1100 and 1300 models could be confused at the time). Sergeant Brian Titmuss who was on duty in the Control Room glanced at the clock as the call came in from D.C. Coward came in. It was 5.55pm.

At this point Skingle got out of the 1300 saloon, walked back to the Police car and stood by the detective as he waited for a reply. Both criminals must have been acutely aware of their situation and what would happen to them when the result of that radio check came through from the Control Room. It would reveal to the Policeman that the registration number was false and that therefore the car was, in all probability, stolen. The detective would call for back up and they would be arrested. In a very short time the Police would not only confirm their suspicions concerning the 1300 but on looking through the car would soon discover the guns in it. Then their true identities would be ascertained and the knowledge that they were abscondees from a prison day release scheme. They would, eventually, be charged with the serious offences committed since they had absented themselves from the pre-release scheme, for which they would receive long prison terms bearing in mind their previous records. They would be unlikely to qualify for any form of parole for many years ahead as they had either broken out of or had absconded from Prison before and they had committed several serious crimes whilst they had been out. Skingle and Sparrow both knew that they were facing years of incarceration. They were indeed two extremely desperate and violent men, armed to the teeth with only one brave and unarmed Policeman between them and freedom.

Whilst this incident was going on, there were a number of witnesses passing by who could see D.C. Coward checking the two men. They also noticed that one of the men was sitting in the passenger seat of the Policeman's car whilst the other was seen looking through the driver's window. As the message about the stolen car started to filter through on the detective's personal radio there was the sudden noise of a gun being fired, again and again and again. Several people not only heard the repeated shots but also saw what happened. One ten year old boy, who had been travelling in the back of his father's car, had seen the 1300 and the Traveller stationary and the man standing by the window of the unmarked Police car. He later told the Police, "... then I heard shots and looked round. I saw one person in the road with a gun in his hands sort of shooting in the window of the car.... He was shooting with quite a big black gun about six inches long."

A woman riding a motorcycle saw the man with a gun poke it through the window and heard several shots being fired. She also noticed that D.C. Coward was curled up on the driving seat. Not really believing what she had seen she thought at first that the incident was part of a film; tragically it was not.

Another saw the man fire a shot, he thought at the windscreen of the car, then saw him walk back to his own parked car, sticking the gun into his belt.

One man, who happened to get in the way of the fleeing criminals and was kicked by one of them, said afterwards, "All I know is there was a bit of a struggle between the man in the car and the other two men by the car. .... the man in the car was a very brave young man, he was not at all frightened."

The two men were then seen running back to the 1300 saloon after slamming the door of the Traveller on the seriously injured detective. In the rush to escape, the criminals reversed their car into the front of the Police vehicle, causing D.C. Coward to collapse onto the ground.

A member of the public, Alan Maughan, realising that something terrible had taken place, attempted to grab hold of the door handle of the departing 1300 but he was forced to let go. He managed, however, to write down part of the registration number of the vehicle as it made off.

Horrifically injured though he was, Ian Coward attempted to crawl along the road and a student nurse dashed over to him, noticing that he was in a state of severe shock and bleeding from one ear. To another, who rushed to his aid, the Constable whispered, "I'm dying! Take me to hospital!"

An ambulance attended shortly afterwards and conveyed D.C. Coward to hospital where it was discovered that he had been shot nine times, in the head, abdomen, lower back and side. It was a ruthless and determined effort not only to prevent the young Policeman from doing his duty but also to seriously maim him at the same time.

The Police had by now been informed by several people about the incident and rushed to Kings Road.

Meanwhile, in another part of Reading, two men, one dark-haired, the other fair-haired, approached a petrol pump attendant at a garage and asked if he had a can into which they could put some petrol. When the attendant could not find a can, one of the two men suggested a bottle; the reason for their request they told him was that they wanted to clean something. To the attendant they both appeared to be agitated and eager to be on their way. He felt intimidated by them and thought that if he refused to get what they wanted they might turn nasty. Eventually a bucket was picked up by one of the men and it was filled with petrol. After paying from a wad of notes and asking if there was any countryside nearby, both men drove off at high speed in the general direction of Newbury in, the attendant noted, a white or cream car.

A few minutes later the Fire Brigade was alerted to a 1300 saloon on fire in an alleyway off Routh Lane, Tilehurst, in Reading. When they arrived, apart from the intense heat generated by the fire, the firemen had to contend with a continuous banging coming from the inside of the vehicle as ammunition exploded. When the blaze was eventually extinguished several firearms, including an Astra pistol, were recovered from the shell of the car. Most of these weapons were loaded, including the Astra.

Teams of Police Officers were, by now, in attendance at both the Kings Road and Routh Lane areas of Reading. Initially, they were led by Detective Superintendent Davies but eventually Detective Superintendent Joseph Coffey a quietly spoken Irishman, who had originally joined the Oxford City Police, was placed in overall charge of the investigation. A widespread and painstaking enquiry was now under way in the search for the perpetrators of this terrible crime. Each Police Officer realised that every clue, no matter how infinitesimal, was needed if they were to track down the ruthless attackers of Ian Coward.

Consequently, as detectives sought out witnesses, the areas where the shooting and the car fire had occurred were examined most thoroughly by Scenes of Crimes Officers under the direction of Detective Chief Inspector John White. What was left of the attacker's car was also methodically searched and the meticulous care with which this was done paid dividends, for, amongst the smouldering remains of the 1300, was found a charred wallet with a letter written on prison notepaper and addressed to one William Arthur Skingle.

Also recovered was the burnt out personal radio belonging to D.C. Coward, which had been snatched from his hands as he performed one of his last acts as a Policeman.

A quick search of records disclosed not only Skingle's terrible record and the fact that he had absconded from the Pentonville pre-release scheme but also the address of his father at 27, Gilbert Grove, Mill

Hill in London. Also revealed was the fact that an equally dangerous criminal, Peter George Sparrow, had also absented himself from the pre-release hostel. Consequently Sergeant Jackson and other detectives of the Regional Crime Squad went to Skingle's father's house and waited apprehensively to see if his nefarious son would show up there. They did not have to wait long, for at 5am on Tuesday, June 29th the doorbell was rung and Sergeant Jackson answered it. As he opened the door he saw that the caller was a young man, very tall, wearing a corduroy jacket and grey trousers and in his stockinged feet! Sergeant Jackson, mindful of the violence shown to his colleague just days before, quickly grabbed hold of him, brought him into the house and held him against the wall.

"What's your name?" he demanded.

"What's it to you, John?" was the immediate reply.

Detective Sergeant Jackson was in no mood to be trifled with and, after informing the young man that he was a Police Officer, he rather forcefully asked him his name once more and what he was doing at this address this early in the morning.

He had come to the house, he informed the detective, because he, "... knew the old man here."

After a quick search of the prisoner and his clothing, D.S. Jackson took him into the front room of the house. As he entered the room the early caller put his hand in his right hand pocket. Another Police Officer present, Sergeant Bailey grasped his arm in a vice like grip.

"Look," the man said, "you might as well know my name is Sparrow. I've got some cartridges in here." D.S. Bailey took 10 shotgun cartridges form his jacket pocket.

D.S. Jackson then asked Sparrow where the shotgun was and he replied, "It's in the car outside." The vehicle was quickly searched and the shotgun, which had been stolen from the school armoury, was found in a plastic bag, both barrels having been shortened. As the detectives looked at it they realised that if this weapon had been fired at close range it would have had devastating results.

Sparrow was asked if he had seen the national papers, especially the headlines concerning the shooting of Ian Coward. He became aggressive, his eyes were blazing and he wagged his finger at the Detective Sergeant Jackson, "Look, John," he replied, "I am not having that one as well. Billy Skingle shot that ******* copper in Reading the other night. He did it, not me. I never got out of the car. I saw him shooting the copper in the head and all over."

He had to admit, however, that being at the scene when D.C. Coward was shot made him as guilty as the actual perpetrator.

Later, when D.S. Jackson had asked him who had set fire to the car, Sparrow had replied, "Look, John, I'm getting fed up with you bastards. I ******* told you there was two of us in Reading, me and Billy Skingle. One of us shot that ******* copper and it was not me. I tell you. He was a hard bastard. He must be if he is still alive."

Detective Sergeant Bailey enquired why he had the cartridges on him, to which Sparrow answered, "I always carry them."

He then said that he and Skingle had split up in Reading after they had burnt the car and that he had not seen Skingle since.

When asked if the gun was the one from Croydon, Sparrow admitted that it was.

Sparrow was taken to Mill Hill Police Station where he was questioned by Detective Superintendent Davies. Sparrow could not remember where they had got the guns from, but agreed that it had looked like a school. He added that they had taken the car from a garage at Heathfield. "We ponced about and then went up to Scotland," he added. He told Superintendent Davies that the guns had all been in the car, one of them in the glove compartment. Sparrow knew that Skingle was violent. "What happened then? queried the Superintendent, referring to the shooting at Reading.

"I was lost and got out of the car. I didn't know the copper was there."

Then D.C. Coward had turned up and asked him if he was all right. "We were standing outside and he asked for identification. I took him to the boot. He took the number and went to his own car. He had a walkie talkie, he was walking up and down and he said, 'Come into the car. I want you to identify yourself.' Then he went to the driver's seat and I went into the passenger's seat and Skingle shot him half in and half out."

Superintendent Davies then asked Sparrow if he had spoken to Skingle.

"When I came from the back, I said to Skingle, 'He wants some identification."

The Superintendent went on, "You knew he was armed."

Sparrow replied, "I didn't know he was going to do that."

Interviewed at Reading Police Station, Sparrow made a statement in which he admitted being the driver of the car in Reading on the 29th June. "Bill" he added, "had one of the guns in the front and the others were in the back on the floor of the car. This Policeman stopped behind us. He came over to me and said he was a Policeman. He asked me if I was all right and said I wasn't driving very straight. I told him I had just been cut up by a bloke.

"The Policeman" he continued, " went to his own car after I'd been with him to the boot of the car to search my stuff for identification. He told me all he wanted was some identification and told me to sit in the passenger seat of the car. He was listening to something on his radio, something about the number of the car or something. As I went to pull the door open I heard a bang and saw Skingle with the gun. I saw the gun was pointed at the Policeman's stomach. As I ran towards our car, I heard four bangs. Bill ran up and got into the passenger seat. I said, "What did you want to do that for?" He said, "He was coming for me." I think he meant he was coming for him because he had seen the gun in Bill's hand."

They had then bought some petrol and changed their clothes and had left everything else behind. "I put a piece of petrol soaked rag in the petrol filler cap." Skingle, he said, had looked back and had seen the flames coming from the car. Skingle had then taken the detective's radio set and had dropped it in the bucket of petrol. Sparrow had last seen it on top of the car. "Bill told me he wasn't going to let anyone take him. The last I saw of him he was running across the fields."

Sparrow continued that he made good his escape, initially going to Bristol, then the following day to Sussex where he had hidden the shotgun. He had then gone to another part of Sussex and had got a car, the same one he had when he was arrested. He had kept a gun, he told the Police, because he was frightened that Skingle might go after him, knowing that he was the only witness. "I knew he was very vicious. I thought he might do me."

He had not stopped Skingle shooting the detective, he added, "...because I might get one in the guts."

It was, of course, of the utmost importance that Skingle be arrested as well and as soon as possible and to this end Superintendent Coffey conferred with Detective Chief Inspector Sugrue, a fellow Irishman, of the Metropolitan Police Flying Squad, and sent 35 detectives from the Thames Valley Constabulary area to assist the Flying Squad. A quite unusual step for the time was that a description of Skingle with his tattoos and his photograph was given to the media for circulation as wanted in connection with the attempted murder of Ian Coward. Anywhere that Skingle might be - clubs, gambling dens, brothels etc. - were visited by Police acting almost as avenging angels for one of their own. The 'underworld' did not like Police Officers being killed or seriously injured by 'rogue' criminals as it brought the wrath of their fellow Policemen down on them as they searched for the perpetrators of such a crime. Detectives tend to leave no stone unturned in their hunt for such men and all sorts of shady deals and ventures are interrupted and exposed to the scrutiny of the Police. There is little rest until the culprit or culprits are arrested and 'business as normal' can be resumed amongst the criminal element. Professional criminals quickly tire of being continually harassed at their homes at odd hours of the day and night or at the places of leisure such as gambling clubs where they tend to congregate and where they meet 'friends' and discuss matters they do not wish the Police to know about. It is especially upsetting where the Police, instead of knocking politely when they wish to gain entry to a house or club, use a sledgehammer instead.

Under these circumstances it was not long before the Flying Squad received the inevitable 'tip off'. Skingle was staying at the Belgrave Hotel, Argyle Square in the Kings Cross area of London. In the early hours of Wednesday, 30th June, a number of Police Officers, three of them armed with revolvers and led by Detective Chief Inspector Sugrue, surrounded the hotel. Quietly, they made their way to room 31 where they could see a light on. At a given word Detective Sergeant Looney forced the door open and he and Detective Sergeant Jenkins rushed into the room where they found their quarry lying on the bed. As the armed Police entered the room Skingle jumped up and a violent struggle ensued until he was overpowered. Realising that some of the Police were armed, Skingle pathetically pleaded, "Don't shoot me! Don't shoot me!" [1] Ian Coward of course had not been given the option. When matters had calmed down, Chief Inspector Sugrue informed his prisoner that he was being arrested for the shooting of a Police Officer the previous Sunday. Skingle replied, "I knew you'd catch up with me. I panicked and let him have it. Please don't shoot me and I'll tell you what happened... it's no good lying to you. I did it. After he stopped us we decided we'd have to do him or get nicked. When I saw he was using a walkie-talkie I told him to put it down but he wouldn't, he still wanted to have a go. I went potty and emptied the gun into him. I deserve topping for shooting that copper. We decided we didn't want to be taken by the law because we thought we were wanted for holding up a geezer."

He then told the detective that the gun used on Ian Coward had been an Astra and he took the arresting detectives to the grounds of Edgware Hospital where another weapon stolen from the school

[1] One is reminded of the capture of George 'Machine gun' Kelly, a notorious American gangster of the 1920s and 1930s, who, when apprehended by the Federal Bureau of Investigation on 26th September 1933, for kidnapping, pleaded with the arresting agents, "Don't shoot G-men! Don't shoot G-men!"

armoury had been secreted, together with 100 rounds of ammunition hidden in a tin.

Taken back to Reading to be charged with the attempted murder of Ian Coward, who was still fighting for his life, Skingle had to be smuggled into the Police Station via a back door to avoid a hostile crowd that had gathered to express their disgust that such a vile act had taken place in the town. Ian Coward was a well known and respected Police Officer in the community.

Both Skingle and Sparrow were charged with his attempted murder.

On Friday, July 23rd, after almost a month's fight against tremendous odds, Ian Coward succumbed to his terrible injuries. He became the first Thames Valley Police Officer to have been killed in the execution of his duty. Skingle and Sparrow were duly charged with his murder.

PART TWO

In October both men were brought up at the Oxfordshire Assizes. In addition to the main charge they were also jointly charged with burglary and theft of firearms and ammunition at a school armoury, armed robbery, burglary and theft of a car and shortening the length of a double barrelled shotgun. Appearing with them was Peter Cox who had been charged with lesser offences. Skingle and Sparrow pleaded not guilty to murder but guilty to the other offences. The Attorney General, the Right Hon. Sir Peter Rawlinson QC, later Baron Rawlinson of Ewell, with Mr Michael Underhill QC and Mr Brian Gibson, prosecuted.

The case for the prosecution was outlined. "It was a cold blooded and brutal murder," declaimed Sir Peter. "It was in the early evening of a June day earlier this year in broad daylight in the public streets of Reading that a young Police Officer was shot. Nine bullets at close range were pumped into his head and body. The gun, which it is alleged was used, was not an automatic but required nine pressures of the finger to fire it. The first bullet probably hit the Police Officer in the head and thereafter eight more shots were fired. It was only when there were no more bullets to fire...that the shooting ceased." Sir Peter went on to describe the tragic sequence of events that led to the eventual death of Ian Coward, the attempts by members of the public to stop the two men from escaping, the setting fire to the stolen car and the arrests of the prisoners. Mr Douglas Draycott QC who was representing Skingle said that his client admitted being a passenger in the white 1300 on June 27th until 3.30pm but not thereafter.

The witnesses for the prosecution were heard, telling of the shooting in Reading and the capture of Sparrow then Skingle, all bearing out the events that had been narrated in the opening speech.

A statement made by Skingle to the investigating detectives was then read out to the hushed Court. "It was me that shot the Police Officer in Reading last Sunday," he had admitted. Both he and Sparrow had apparently been travelling around the country "... looking for places to screw. Then we decided to go to Devon." The pair of them had reached Reading with Sparrow driving and cutting up other road users. "We had a ruck with the driver of another car and we were pulled up by a geezer who said he was a copper." He had asked Sparrow for some identification and had then gone back to his own car talking into his personal radio. Sparrow, according to Skingle's statement, had been standing by the side of the Police car and had then come back to theirs (the stolen 1300). Sparrow had allegedly said "... it looks like a run out and it's all on top."

The statement went on, "We had agreed that if we were pulled by the law we would hold him up and take his radio and keys and take him somewhere where he could not get near a phone and leave him stranded. This is what we meant by a run out." Carrying on in the statement, Skingle had said that Sparrow had returned to the Police car and had got inside. "I went to the driver's side and the copper was talking on the radio. I took the revolver from my waistband and pointed it at him. I said, "Don't move and nothing will happen." He dropped one bit of the radio and struck at the gun with the other bit of the radio and tried to grab the gun with his other hand. I pulled back and pulled the trigger. I could see that the bullet had hit him in the head. He still kept fighting with me and kicking out at me. He wasn't worried about the gun, he was a brave bastard, I give him that. I panicked and kept pulling the trigger and I know I emptied the gun into him and after that he was still fighting like a maniac. He was still trying to talk into the radio and I had to fight him to get it off him and ran back to the car."

The statement then went on to recount how, after the shooting, Skingle and Sparrow had bought some petrol before they had driven some yards up a path. They had then changed their clothes and Sparrow had taken a scarf, doused it in the petrol and had stuck one end in the tank and the other in the boot of the stolen car and had then set the car alight, having already soaked it in petrol. The two men had then run off. Sparrow had suggested that they split up which they did and Skingle had returned to London by train. He had gone to his home and watched Police Five but there had been nothing on the programme about the shooting. He had then left his parents' home and had booked a room in the Belgrave Hotel where he had later been arrested.

Detective Sergeant Jim Auger of the Thames Valley Constabulary, giving evidence, related that he had spoken to Skingle when he had been in a cell at Reading Police Station after he had made the statement and had asked him if he had anything further to say. Skingle had answered, "No, except that I did the shooting. It's no good saying sorry now."

Sergeant Auger asserted that Skingle had then said that after Sparrow had been speaking to Detective Constable Coward he had returned to their car and had asked for a gun. "I wouldn't give it to him. I thought he might do the copper. I then go and do what I stopped him doing."

D.S. Auger also stated that when he showed Skingle the guns recovered from the burnt out car, he had picked out the Astra pistol which had been used in the fatal shooting of the detective. Sparrow had done likewise.

Two more statements were then read out to the Court. The first was that of Mr Norman Rothney, the consultant surgeon who had examined Detective Constable Coward on his admission to Battle Hospital. The Officer was suffering from severe shock he stated, from the abdominal haemorrhage caused by the bullets which had lodged in his stomach. Another bullet had passed through his neck and had come to rest in his jaw. Altogether nine bullets were found in the Detective's body. D.C. Coward was later removed to the Royal Berkshire Hospital where he had seemed to improve but then he deteriorated and he finally died at 4.25pm on July 23rd.

Mr George Price, a Home Office Forensic Scientist, had examined the Detective's clothing. There were, he said, eight bullet entrance holes in his jacket on the right hand side which were consistent with a gun having been fired at close range. "The muzzle of the weapon was in approximate contact with the jacket when fired," he said.

That concluded the case for the prosecution and it was now the turn of the defence lawyers.

Mr Stephen Brown QC, for Sparrow, caused a minor sensation when he said that he did not propose calling any witnesses and it was Skingle who now entered the witness box. What he had to say was a complete rejection of the evidence that he was the killer. He admitted that he, Sparrow and Cox had gone to the school in Croydon, had broken into the armoury and had stolen firearms and ammunition and these were the exhibits produced before the Court by the prosecution. He described how he and Sparrow had shortened the barrels of the shotgun when they were staying in Brighton. They had then stolen the car and had journeyed to Scotland, stopping en route to try out the guns in a disused quarry in Westmorland. They had continued on to

Scotland where they had met a man in a cafe who had taken them to a furnished room where they had been introduced to Peter Knox, known as 'Knoxie'. The three of them, after discussing matters, had then travelled down to the South of England.

Mr Draycott moved his client on to the day of the shooting. Skingle said that the three of them had set off in the white 1300 with the intention of travelling to Devon. The guns were either in the front of the car or in the boot. There was, according to Skingle, a feeling of mutual hatred between the three men although Knox and Sparrow appeared to be getting on reasonably well. Arguments were occurring all the time, he alleged, and such was the atmosphere in the car that when he got out at Boreham Wood to check a signpost the car had been driven off, leaving him stranded with his overcoat at the side of the road. He had then walked back to London via a cafe near Pentonville Prison, where he had bought an ounce of cannabis. After watching television at his parents' house, he had gone to a West End club where he had stayed until the early hours. On Tuesday (29th June), he had seen Sparrow and he had asked him where the rest of his clothes were. Sparrow had told him that they had been burnt when the car had been set on fire.

Sparrow had also told him about the encounter with Detective Constable Coward and of how Knox had threatened the detective with a gun and had then shot him. After setting fire to the car, Sparrow and Knox had split up, Knox having returned to Scotland. Sparrow, Skingle related, wanted help but he had refused as he had, in his opinion, stolen his clothes and then burnt them, leaving him stranded.

Why, he was asked, had he gone to the West End at the time? Skingle answered that he had felt hungry and had gone to his parents' home but a warning signal that he had arranged with his parents, a milk bottle usually left in a flowerpot, was missing. As he walked past the house he could not see a milk bottle in either pot so he had carried on.

He was asked by his counsel why he was so anxious to avoid contact with the Police. "Because I was on the run from Pentonville Prison," he replied.

Skingle said that although he had no intention of helping Sparrow he had said that he would and told him to go to his parents' house and tell his father to put him up. He was to say that he, Skingle, would be home in a couple of days as soon as he had finished some business that he had to attend to. Skingle knew that the Police were already there because of the warning signal and he now admitted in Court that he had sent Sparrow there in order that he would be arrested. He, meanwhile, had gone to The Belgrave Hotel where he had smoked cannabis and drunk whisky until his room had been entered by a lot of Policemen, some carrying truncheons and some guns. He had been told not to move by one of them.

Mr Draycott asked his client, "Did you move?"

Skingle sneered, "You're joking! With all those guns and sticks. I certainly didn't. I screamed and screamed, 'Don't shoot me!' I nearly died of fright when I saw that lot."

After having been handcuffed he had taken the arresting officers to Burnt Oak where he had hidden a gun. He had then been conveyed to Cannon Row Police Station where he had made a statement denying the offence.

Mr Draycott intervened, "The Police Officers say that no statement was made at Cannon Row Police Station."

"Yes," responded Skingle, "because in the first statement I denied I had done it. This doesn't suit their purpose. Of course they are going to deny this statement exists."

He had then been driven to Reading Police Station where he had been charged. He was asked if anything had occurred in the car taking him to Reading.

"Sugrue turned to me and said, 'Up to now we are only Policemen and a Policeman has been shot. These blokes there are his mates, so unless you are going to co-operate there isn't much hope.' ...I decided to co-operate. I made a statement. I knew the Police Officer was only wounded. He knew who shot him... Sooner or later he would come forward and say, 'That's not the man who shot me.'

He was asked by his counsel if, when he had been charged with D.C. Coward's murder, he had told the Police that a man called Knox had done it and that a dreadful mistake had been made. Skingle acknowledged that he had not.

The Attorney General now rose to cross-examine the man in the witness box.

He opened by asking why had he stolen the weapons from the armoury.

"Because I was interested in guns," was the rejoinder.

"What did you want them for?"

"For sport," explained Skingle.

"What did you intend to use those guns for?"

"There was no specific reason," Skingle answered. "Sparrow wanted them, I wanted them and Peter Cox wanted them. I wasn't interested in the shotgun, Sparrow claimed that."

Sir Peter pressed on determinedly, "What do you think he wanted that shotgun for?"

Skingle replied somewhat resignedly, "He could have wanted it for a lot of things. I didn't ask."

"What do you think he wanted it for?"

Skingle replied off-handedly, "Perhaps sport, perhaps robbery."

Sir Peter held up the sawn off shotgun for Skingle and all in the court, especially the jury, to see. "What is the advantage in having a gun modified like this?" he queried, knowing there could only be but one answer.

"I would say it's no good for anything but crime," Skingle had to admit.

The Attorney General kept relentlessly on, "Was the sole purpose for taking those guns to use them for crime?"

"Nine guns? Taking on an army?" was the contemptuous reply.

"Why did you take all that ammunition?"

"If you use it for sport you need a lot of rounds. If you use it for robbery you only need a handful."

Sir Peter skilfully took him through his evidence of how he had 'banged off' about five hundred rounds when they had tried out the guns on the way to Scotland and that he had used the Astra first.

"Did you," enquired Sir Peter, " have a pistol in your pocket?"

"I had three or four loaded guns in the front of the car. Almost all the time I was in that car there were three or four loaded guns in the front."

"Within literally touching distance from where you were sitting. Why did you have these guns in that position, loaded?"

"We were going up north and we wanted to take them with us. For most of the time there was a gun in the pocket of the door. The same on the driver's side. And I had one or two under the seat."

"Was the purpose in having them there so that you could get at them quickly if you were stopped?"

"No!"

"Did you think you might be stopped?"

"Not really. What is the good of having a loaded gun in the car if a Policeman stops you. What are you going to do? Shoot the copper when all you have to do is run in the opposite direction of the Police car?"

The Attorney General then queried why they had kept guns in the car on the way back from Scotland when 'Knoxie' was with them.

Skingle had to concede,"Basically the three of us are all thieves."

Asked why he had kept ammunition in his pocket, Skingle responded, "I had got a gun. I like it. I am happy with it." He was forced to admit that he was determined that he would not be taken but would have 'legged it' if a Policeman had kept coming for him when he had a gun. He would first, though, have fired a shot in the air as a threat.

"Of course, Detective Constable Coward had still kept coming."

"I don't know. I wasn't there."

"It is a very brave man, is it not, who attempts to fight off a person with a gun at point blank range and an even braver man who keeps on even after he has been shot?" Sir Peter Rawlinson put to him.

"Yes, especially then."

When he was questioned regarding the statement he had made based upon what Sparrow had told him had occurred, he had, he said, added his own imaginative details as a 'filler sweetener', that was what the Police had wanted. He had probably told Detective Chief Inspector Sugrue that he had shot D.C. Coward but he had done this to lead him to believe that he, Skingle, was admitting it. He had made it, he said, because of his ill treatment at the hands of the Police.

The Court adjourned at this point and when it resumed on the next day, the seventh day of the trial, Skingle returned to the witness box where he had already spent four hours answering questions from both his counsel and the prosecution.

The Attorney General continued by asking Skingle if he had read in the newspapers about the two men, who might be armed and who were wanted in connection with the shooting.

Skingle said that he had.

"Did you read about the hunt for a man with a tattoo? Hold up your hand!" Sir Peter demanded, "What have you got there?"

Skingle did as he was told, replying at the same time, "A tattoo." He also acknowledged that he had a further tattoo on his other hand with some writing.

"Did you think you might be wanted for questioning?"

"Yes. I have met thousands of crooks in my life but never met any with the same tattoos."

The Attorney General paused to let the jury absorb this before tackling Skingle on another matter. "Why did you not tell the Police Officers about the man Knox?"

"It would not have done me any good. I would have got a good hiding," was the lame response.

"If Knox exists, the Police would have gone for him," Sir Peter persisted.

"They wanted me. I was not permitted. I was not allowed. They didn't want to hear it," Skingle blustered.

The Attorney General sat down and Skingle returned to the dock after almost five hours in the witness box.

There was one other witness called by the defence, John Edward Merry, who straightaway had to confess that he was serving six years imprisonment for perjury! This was for what he had told a Court in a divorce case. He testified that he knew Sparrow, having spent several months with him in prison where he had told Merry that he intended to rob a bank in Scotland. He added that Sparrow had told him that he and another had also planned to carry out a series of armed robberies, saying that if he was ever caught on one of them he was never going to be taken; he would shoot the copper rather than be arrested.

When he was cross-examined, Merry denied that he had been lying nor that he had requested Sparrow to assist him in escaping from prison.

In his final speech, Sir Peter Rawlinson addressed the jury in those mellifluous tones that had been heard in many Courts and in several debates in the House of Commons. He reminded them that Detective Constable Coward, after being riddled with bullets, made a brave attempt to grab the gun from the man Skingle whom the Crown alleged was the murderer. "You may think Skingle was lying in the witness box as coldly as he shot Detective Constable Coward. You have heard an ugly and vicious story whatever verdict you may come to. It required a cold purpose to be able to do this. It was not a shooting done in the panic of pursuit but of a seated man in a car."

Mr Brown, for Sparrow, pointed out that the prosecution had to prove that his client believed and knew that Skingle was going to fire that gun at that time and place. "In my submission the evidence falls short of that. Sparrow's statement seriously implicated him but there was no reason not to doubt that it was what had occurred. Sparrow had not been carrying a gun when he went to the car. The shooting happened 'in a flash' before he could grasp what was happening."

Mr Draycott now rose and pointed out that his client, Skingle, had never been identified as the man at the scene of the shooting although there had been fifteen people there, and moreover no description given by the witnesses fitted Skingle and there was no forensic evidence to connect him to the scene of the crime, no fingerprints, nothing. "Do you think," he earnestly beseeched the jury, "Skingle could have stood and fired a gun nine times in the presence of witness after witness and not be recognised?"

Moving on to the statements Skingle had made to the Police, Mr Draycott added, "When you have got statements and admissions in issue you should look at the rest of the case and ask yourselves, 'What evidence is there that Skingle was at the scene of the crime?'"

The Judge, Mr Justice Stephen Chapman, in his summing up, praised the tremendous courage of Ian Coward for fighting on even though he had received nine bullet wounds. "One cannot read or hear the evidence which you, the jury, have heard without feeling sympathy with his family and a feeling of a sense of real horror that any person should treat an unarmed Police Officer in such an appalling manner. How this man fought like a maniac...is almost beyond comprehension. It shows the tremendous courage the man had." However, Mr Justice Chapman warned the jury not to let their emotions cloud their judgement.

After deliberating for almost four hours the jury returned with a verdict of 'Guilty ' against both Skingle and Sparrow.

Mr Justice Chapman addressed Skingle first, "It is quite obvious from your record that you set yourself at an early age to be an enemy of society. You are a highly dangerous man who resorts to violence without any compunction or hesitation whatever. You were the person who pulled the trigger of that gun on the Police Officer on that evening in June. A Policeman is an Officer of the law in the sense that he is appointed to protect the rights, liberties, property and person of the individual citizen in all circumstances and at whatever the cost. To shoot down such a man while he is performing these duties in a legal, decent and proper manner and not merely by firing one shot but shot after shot after shot is, in my view the ultimate in criminality. The law only allows me to pass sentence of imprisonment for life and in my view, having indicated the ultimate in criminality, it can only bear the ultimate in punishment, if the words are to have meaning and the law to make any sense. My recommendation to the Home Secretary will be that those dreadful words I have just used should have their awful dreadful meaning. In other words, life should mean life."

The judge now passed on to Sparrow, who also asked the Court to take into consideration five further offences of taking cars. "I have given very anxious consideration to the question of what recommendation I should make in your case. You also have an appalling record, including violence and use of firearms. The criminality in your case is the same, even though you did not fire the shots that killed that Police Officer. But I do think the fact that you were not actually firing the gun should make some difference in my recommendation to the Home Secretary. I think I am justified in not making such a drastic recommendation as in the case of Skingle. The recommendation in your case will be 25 years."

In respect of the other matters in which they had pleaded guilty, Mr Justice Chapman sentenced them to a total of thirty years imprisonment to run concurrent with their life sentences.

The jury, after giving their verdict, had praised Alan Maughan "for the considerable bravery he showed in attempting to tackle the two men after the shooting." Mr. Justice Chapman endorsed their remarks and also praised the Police Officers in the case for their considerable courage and gallantry.

Detective Superintendent Joseph Coffey, at the conclusion of the case, immediately went to the Chief Constable of the Thames Valley Constabulary to report on the outcome of the case and to request that the Judge's commendation was not entered on the investigating officers' records of service. "We had done what we had to do in the pursuit of the murderers of a colleague and did not wish to be praised in any way for doing so."[2]

Ian Coward was awarded, posthumously, the Queen's Medal for Gallantry. Mrs Coward still lives in the Reading area and has worked at the local Police Station for several years as secretary to successive Chief Superintendents. Matthew, the son of Ian and Mrs Coward, is now a research chemist putting the final touches to a Ph.D.[3]

Joseph Coffey was later promoted to Chief Superintendent in overall charge of No.5 Regional Crime Squad, awarded the Queen's Police Medal for Distinguished Service and, after a long and successful career in the Police, mainly in the Criminal Investigation Department, eventually retired from the Police Service.

Arthur William Skingle died in Full Sutton Prison.

Peter George Sparrow was released from prison after serving 27 years.

Patrick Sugrue retired from the Metropolitan Police in 1980 and died in 1993.

2 *Letter to author.* 3 *Letter to author.*

Mrs Gillian Coward proudly receives her late husband's medal for gallantry.

ONE DREADFUL DAY IN HUNGERFORD

POLICE CONSTABLE ROGER BRERETON
Thames Valley Police - 1987

Hungerford, that small, bustling West Berkshire town that borders Wiltshire, has had its fair share of history. The Romans soldiers, merchants and administrators - travelled past on their way to Aquae Sulis, or, as we know it better, Bath, although the main highway, the 'Bath Road', which now snakes through part of Hungerford was, until 1744, diverted through Chilton Foliat past Littlecote Park to Ramsbury and Marlborough. By an Act of Parliament that year the road, also now known rather prosaically as the A4, was altered to go through to Froxfield and the nearby Savernake Forest.

In November 1643, during the Civil War, King Charles I made The Bear Inn at Hungerford his headquarters for three days. In 1688, after King James II's troops had been defeated at Reading, emissaries from that King came to see Prince William of Orange whilst he rested, also at The Bear Inn, after his advance from landing at Brixham. King James' commissioners sought an audience with the Prince and a letter was handed to him from the monarch. The meeting and the events that followed led to the eventual flight of the last Jacobean king.

Samuel Pepys, the diarist, also stayed at Hungerford and in the eighteenth century travellers from London stopped here on their way to Bath, now made fashionable by Beau Nash, to sample the waters and probably much else besides. They too called at The Bear Inn, as did the Hanoverian Kings, Lord Nelson and Beau Brummell among others.

It was also at the junction of the Bath Road (here called Charnham Street) and Bridge Street on which this hostelry stands, that in 1876 Inspector Drewitt of the Berkshire Constabulary chatted to a

Wiltshire Constable before going on to meet P.C. Shorter and their fatal encounter with poachers at nearby Folly Crossroads.

Bridge Street, which leads into the town proper from this junction, traverses the Kennet and Avon Canal and is in turn surmounted by the Railway Bridge that now carries the successors to Brunel's magnificent Great Western Railway to and from London and the West Country. Just a few yards farther on lies Park Street, a narrow road in which the town Police Station is located. This fine Victorian edifice, erected in the 1860s, has, outwardly at least, changed little since that December night when Inspector Drewitt set out on his last patrol.

One would think that would be enough history for such a beautiful, small country town but in the late twentieth century it unfortunately nurtured a veritable viper within its breast.

By the 1980s the Berkshire Constabulary had vanished into history, amalgamated, in the 1960s, with four other Police forces to form the Thames Valley Constabulary, later amended to the Thames Valley Police. Policemen still worked from Hungerford's nineteenth century Police Station but now they went forth mainly in cars rather than on foot or by cycle.

One of the many recruits who had joined the newly created Thames Valley Police in 1973 was Roger Brereton who had just left the Royal Navy. The 1970s were a turbulent decade for the British Police as they struggled to cope with anarchists, terrorists, rioters and an ever-increasing crime rate. It also proved to be lean times for the Police as their salaries failed to keep up with inflation and, for the first time since 1919, there was talk of Policemen striking for better pay. Banned by their constitution from taking such drastic action, many officers decided to vote with their feet instead and chose to leave the Police Service for better paid jobs elsewhere. However, those who joined and who weathered the storms of those tumultuous years showed commitment to their chosen profession.

101

Having served in the Royal Navy for a number of years, Police Constable 1429 Brereton, as he now became, would have brought a wealth of experience with him and a more mature outlook on life than some who would need to have the 'rough edges smoothed away'. Married with two small children, after initial training he was posted to Wantage, another ancient Berkshire town, celebrated as the birthplace of Alfred the Great, the 'founder' of the Royal Navy. Whether P.C. Brereton paused to think of the irony of such a posting is not known as he patrolled the streets of the town.

Police Constable Roger Brereton. (Thames Valley Police)

He was then sent to Hungerford and after a while re-assigned to the Traffic Department, working from their Newbury base. Now he would specialise in Road traffic matters rather than the mundane day to day tasks of a beat Constable. He would be attempting to prevent the public at large from committing carnage on the highways. Dealing with serious, sometimes fatal accidents, reporting and no doubt at times issuing a warning or friendly 'caution' to errant motorists as they sped along the A4, the M4 and other roads in Berkshire in an effort to make the highways safer for all users.

Roger also took a great interest in aiding the widows and orphans of the Royal Ulster Constabulary, whose members were under sustained attack by various factions of the Irish Republican Army and 'Loyalist' terrorists throughout the 1970s and 1980s.

On Wednesday, 19th August 1987 on what would have seemed to be just another tour of duty, P.C. Brereton reported at Newbury Police Station at 8am. It appeared as if it would be an ordinary day, not only for Police in Newbury and Hungerford but also for Policemen and women everywhere throughout the Thames Valley Police district and indeed the rest of the country.

Some hours later another man set out from Hungerford and drove west to the Savernake Forest. His name was Michael Ryan and he was an enigmatic man of 27 years of age who lived with his mother in a house in the town, his father having died some years before. He was a strange man, a loner; a man given to fantasising. He would invent stories about himself, whilst his mother, for some reason, backed him up. He spread a tale around the district of how he had met a Colonel some years before who was his beneficiary. This gentleman was allegedly a millionaire who lived on an estate at Thatcham in Berkshire. He was supposed to own a plane, a helicopter and tanks. He had allegedly given Ryan a Porsche car and allowed him to reside in a cottage within the grounds of his estate. None of these claims nor any other, such as having served in the Armed forces or that he had a connection with any other Military organisation, were found to be true when investigated later by the Police. They were all part of a make believe world in which he lived.

However, what was real was that Ryan had an abiding love for guns and not only possessed but also acquired and got rid of a number of firearms over the course of years. By August of 1987 he owned a Kalashnikov 7.62 rifle, a 9mm Beretta pistol, .30 Ml Underwood carbine and, it is believed, several shotguns.

On 19th August Ryan drove around the vast Savernake Forest and noticed a parked car, with a mother and two children busy having a picnic. As they finished and began tidying away Ryan got out of his car, a Vauxhall Astra, and strolled over to where Mrs Sue Godfrey, a petite woman of thirty-five, had been giving her children a treat prior to visiting her grandmother at North Newnton in Wiltshire that afternoon. Ryan pointed his Beretta at Mrs Godfrey and ordered her to place the children into her car. When she had done that Ryan marched her off some distance into the forest, carrying a groundsheet with him. Suddenly there was the sound of shots and the children saw Ryan run back to his car and drive hurriedly off.

His next call was at the Golden Arrow Service Station on the Bath Road at Froxfield. Ryan was a regular caller and Mrs Kakoub Dean, the wife of the proprietor, was not unduly surprised to see his car draw up at a petrol pump. What Ryan did next more than surprised Mrs. Dean, for he fired a gun at her and a bullet narrowly missed her. Ryan now came inside the garage, as if to finish the job off. Terrified, Mrs Dean lay under the counter, appealing to Ryan for mercy. She heard the sound of several clicks, Ryan's gun was empty and he fled from the scene. Mrs Dean realised that she had had a lucky escape from death. Officers from the Wiltshire Constabulary, on receiving the report of Sue Godfrey's murder from another visitor to Savernake Forest, responded immediately. They found her body which had been literally 'riddled with bullets'.

Ryan in the meantime drove back towards Hungerford and parked his car at his home at 4, South View. A neighbour, Mrs Jackson, saw the car draw up and Ryan get out and walk to his home. The look on his face she would later describe as 'fierce'. As she was about to enter her own house she heard the sound of several shots being fired and noticed Ryan running along South View towards her house. Hungerford and its people were about to undergo their ordeal.

Another resident of South View also heard the sound of gunfire and being naturally curious went to see what was going on. As she did so she saw Roland Mason of number 6 in the back yard of his house. She must have been, apart from the killer, the last person to see him alive, for it was about this time that Ryan murdered both Mr Mason and his wife. Ryan continued along South View, appearing to fire indiscriminately as he went. Mrs Jackson, who had seen Ryan return home from his murderous foray into Wiltshire and who was now watching him from what she thought was the safety of her own house, was shot in the back as bullets came in through the window.

At number 13 South View, Lisa Mildenhall, her sister and some friends were playing in the back garden of the house. Hearing gunfire the sisters went to the front door and saw Ryan going along the street. He suddenly stopped as he reached the driveway of their house and fired at them. Lisa Mildenhall, not realising that she had been hit, saw that the front of the trousers that she was wearing was covered in blood. She returned to the kitchen where her mother and a neighbour, who happened to be a member of the St. John's Ambulance Brigade, saw her. Lisa was given attention until she could be removed to hospital later.

Another witness, Mrs Morley, saw Ryan emerge from some gardens and run along South View in the direction of Hungerford Common. It was shortly afterwards that Mr Kenneth Clements, his wife and family, going for a walk along South View towards the Common, encountered Mrs Morley who told them what she had seen. Kenneth Clements now went as fast as he could whilst his son tried to keep up with him. They heard the sound of gunshots and also noticed that a house in South View was on fire. As Kenneth Clements came to the footpath that led to the Common, Ryan emerged from a gateway holding a gun in the upward position. He lowered it and fired. Kenneth Clements was struck and fell to the ground. Ryan deliberately fired several more shots at the fallen figure.

As a result of Ryan's murder of Mrs Godfrey and the attempt on the life of Mrs Dean at the Golden Arrow Garage, Police Officers from both the Wiltshire and Thames Valley forces had been requested to go to the A4 to keep observation for the vehicle in which the attacker had left the scene. As various Police Officers responded, another call came over the radio that an armed man had been seen in South View, Hungerford.

Two of the Policemen who answered these calls were P.C. Roger Brereton and P.C.111 Jeremy Wood. As they drove their separate vehicles as quickly and as safely as they could in the direction of the by now increasingly beleaguered Hungerford, it was decided that P.C. Brereton, in his Motorway patrol car, would enter the town by way of the High Street, whilst his colleague would come from the direction of the Common.

The Control Room of the Thames Valley Police Headquarters at Kidlington stressed that, in view of the seriousness of the calls that were coming in from Hungerford, extreme care should be taken by all Police Officers engaged. The belief was that the offender was still on the rampage in the town and was armed and very dangerous.

Notwithstanding that report, the unarmed P.C. Brereton swept into South View and stopped his vehicle. Ryan came from one of the gardens in the street and, standing in front of the Police car, callously fired at the Policeman striking him several times and fatally wounding him. The last words heard from Roger Brereton by the control room at Kidlington were, "Ten-nine, ten-nine, ten-nine. I've been shot!" With those last, few dramatic words, Kidlington control room realised that the situation was now very grave for the code words 'ten-nine' alone meant that a Police Officer was in personal danger and it was a strict instruction that they were never to be used except in extreme circumstances.

Several people who had seen what had happened in those few seconds in South View also knew just how serious the situation was as they saw P.C. Brereton now slumped, lifeless, across the steering wheel of his car.

P.C.Wood, approaching the Common, had also heard his colleague's, emergency shout over the radio. After that last tragic call nothing else was heard from P.C. Brereton.

Police Constable Jeremy Wood.

P.C.Wood, now joined by other Officers, Sergeant 2172 Ryan and P.C. 2737 Maggs, was approached by Robert Clements, who informed them that his father had been shot. The Policemen bravely attempted to reach Kenneth Clements but they were shot at themselves by Ryan. P.C. Maggs could even see Ryan loading one of his guns.

A Mrs Linda Chapman and her daughter, who had both heard shots being fired, became worried about the horses they kept in a field to the rear of South View. Driving from their home into South View they first of all saw the stationary Police car then, ominously, the figure of Michael Ryan. Looking hard at them he raised a rifle and fired several shots in their direction, striking the grille and windscreen of their Volvo car. Both Mrs Chapman and her daughter were injured; Mrs Chapman in the neck and her daughter in the leg. With great presence of mind, Mrs Chapman reversed her car at speed back along South View into Fairview Road, whilst Ryan continued to fire at the retreating vehicle. They went to the doctor's surgery where both received treatment for their injuries.

An ambulance of the Berkshire Ambulance Service, having been directed to South View, now came under attack as the two women manning the vehicle, Linda Constance Bright and Hazel Jacqueline Haslett, tried to reach the injured. Hazel Haslett received injuries from glass broken by the impact of a bullet. They beat a hasty retreat and shouted a message over their radio set that they had come under fire, before going on to assist other people who had been seriously injured.

Ryan was by now shooting in the direction of a bungalow in Fairview Road owned by Mr Abdur Rahman Khan. He and his wife, Bessie, were working in the rear garden when Mrs Khan, on hearing what she thought were cracking sounds, went to the back gate to investigate, leaving her husband to carry on with the gardening. She heard three more similar sounds and then heard her husband emit a moaning sound and call out, "Bessie, Bessie." Mrs Khan returned to discover her husband lying on his back, with blood staining the front of his clothing and under his left arm. She attempted to make him as comfortable as possible whilst she telephoned for an ambulance. It was all in vain, however, as shortly after Abdur Khan died of his wounds.

After shooting Abdur Khan, Ryan noticed a pedestrian approximately 100 yards from him. Swinging around, he shot at this man, striking him in the arm and knocking him to the ground. As the injured man rose, Ryan fired again; this time the bullet struck the man in the left thigh. The pedestrian managed to make good his escape to a shop nearby, where he was eventually rescued by an ambulance crew.

Mrs Jackson, meanwhile, although injured, had telephoned a friend, George White, asking that he let her husband know what had happened. That gentleman had then driven to Mr Jackson's workplace and collected him, and then they had made for South View. As they turned into the street, Mr Jackson saw the Police patrol car with its driver, Roger Brereton, collapsed in the front.

Almost immediately their car came under intense fire and both men were hit. Their car slammed into the Police vehicle, George White dying almost instantaneously, whilst Ivor Jackson, although seriously injured, realised that he would have to feign death if he was not to be shot at again by his attacker.

At this point, Ryan's mother drove into South View, stopped her car and got out. Mrs Ryan walked past the two men, one dead and the other wounded, she glanced in and muttered, "Oh, Ivor," before running past the Police car after her son, shouting at him, "Michael, Michael, stop it!"

Ryan pointed his rifle at his mother. As she realised what he was about to do, she pleaded, "Don't shoot me!" Ryan fired twice. His mother screamed and fell to the ground, dead.

Ryan, having now added matricide to his crimes, left South View. In his wake he left seven dead and as many injured.

He made his way to Clarks Gardens and a Mrs Tolladay, a resident, having heard the noise, called out to him to stop it. Ryan turned his gun towards her and fired. Mrs Tolladay fell to the ground, injured in the groin. Crawling back into her house she managed to call the emergency services and was eventually, some hours later, taken by ambulance to the Princess Alexandra Hospital at R.A.F. Wroughton.

Ryan walked on towards the Memorial Gardens and the Swimming Pool area. He encountered twenty-six years old Francis Butler, out exercising his dog in the gardens. Ryan raised his gun once again and fired three times. Mr Butler fell, holding his side.

David John Sparrow, a lifeguard and attendant at the swimming pool, on hearing the shots went down to the main entrance of the pool and looked out to the gardens. He saw not only Francis Butler lying on the footpath but also Ryan, with a rifle in each hand making his way towards the main gates. Realising there was not a moment to lose, Sparrow commenced clearing the swimming pool of all the bathers. He then returned to the War Memorial Gardens and, finding that Mr Butler was still alive, went to the office to fetch first aid equipment and help.

At virtually the same time several witnesses either saw or heard the sound of further gunfire as Ryan shot and killed Mr Marcus Barnard, a taxi driver, as he was driving along Bulpit Lane. The killer then emerged from the Memorial Gardens.

Meanwhile people were attempting to aid Francis Butler, who was still lying on the footpath, but notwithstanding their ministrations he died shortly after. While they were trying to help the fatally wounded Mr Butler a rifle, left behind by Ryan, was seen lying on the ground close by and it was later recovered by Police Sergeant Sullivan and taken to Hungerford Police Station.

Ryan was now seen to walk along Bulpit Lane in the direction of Priory Avenue. As he did so he fired at a resident who took cover behind a lorry.

A Mrs Honeybone, who was driving her car along Priory Avenue, was somewhat luckier than others, for as she passed by the junction with Bulpit Lane she heard two shots and the passenger windows of her car were smashed. She received slight cuts to her face, hand and leg.

A stranger to the area, John Storms, a washing machine engineer, was looking for an address in Hungerford Park Farm. He stopped his van in Hillside Road at its junction with Priory Avenue. Glancing to his right he observed Ryan approaching from Priory Avenue. Curiously, he also noticed that Ryan was carrying a rifle. He also saw Ryan adopt a crouching position and point a pistol directly at him. Mr Storm's immediate thought was that the man was fooling about. He was abruptly disabused of this when he heard the sound of a shot, the offside window of his van was smashed and he felt acute pain in his jaw, mouth and neck. Blood poured from his wound and he dropped down into the passenger seat. Mr Storms managed to look above the dashboard of his van and saw Ryan point the gun at him once more and fire off further shots. John Storms was saved from almost certain death when he was rescued by a resident who dashed out and pulled him from his van.

It was at this moment that Mr Douglas Wainwright was driving his Datsun saloon motor car along Priory Avenue towards Hillside Road. Accompanying him was his wife Kathleen. They were on their way to visit their son Trevor, one of the town's Policemen. They chose this precise moment to drive up to Ryan. He turned to their car and started firing into it and the windscreen shattered. Mr Wainwright stopped the car, but Ryan continually shot at the two people inside, injuring Mrs Wainwright but killing her husband. As Ryan reloaded his gun, Mrs Wainwright took the opportunity to get out of the car and run to its rear and crouch down.

Ryan, it was noticed, then walked off along Priory Avenue in the direction of the school. Two other persons were fired on by Ryan as they drove near him, either to be slightly wounded or to be missed altogether. The driver of the last vehicle, Kevin Frederick Lance, who had collected the van he was driving, had been shot in his right arm but managed to drive away from the immediate scene before abandoning the van and making his way back to his works to receive treatment for his wound.

It was at this stage that a Sherpa van, driven by Eric Vardy with Stephen Ball, drove along Tarrants Hill, which adjoins Priory Avenue. The two men saw Kevin Lance running across the road holding his injured arm. Suddenly there was a loud bang. The windscreen of the Sherpa was smashed and there were more bangs. Mr Vardy jumped. The van increased speed and ran through the junction and across Priory Avenue before coming to rest in a hedge. The engine was still racing away and Mr Ball switched it off. Clambering out of the vehicle, Mr Ball ran to a shop for assistance but found that it was closed. He returned to the van and, seeing that his colleague was bleeding profusely from wounds to his jaw and to his side, tore off his 'T' shirt and tried to staunch the flow of blood. He was spurred on as Mr Vardy pleaded for help. An ambulance arrived and took the critically wounded man to a Swindon Hospital but he was pronounced dead upon arrival there.

Ryan re-loaded his gun and continued on,entering Orchard Park Close, where he fired at one house and, although some slight damage was caused, no one was injured, but, when he saw a woman standing in the porchway and he fired in her direction, the bullet, after passing through the door frame, had smacked against her shoe.

Ryan's next victim was to be Sandra Hill. As she drove her Renault saloon along Priory Road he was seen to fire directly at her. The red Renault came slowly to a halt and several men ran to assist the driver who lay slumped across the steering wheel. As carefully as they could they laid her down on the grass verge and someone summoned an ambulance. By the time it had arrived, however, Sandra Hill was dead.

Ryan walked on and went to the front door of number 60 Priory Road. He kicked in the glass panel and walked in. This was the home of Victor and Myrtle Gibbs. A neighbour heard a woman's voice shout out," What the hell do you think you're playing at?" There was the sudden sound of gunfire, screams and then silence. Ryan left the house as he had entered, pausing only to fire once again at a curious neighbour who had also heard the noise and, on looking out to see what had caused the row, had been shot in the leg for her troubles.

The next door neighbour of the Gibbs, on hearing the commotion at number 60, came to the front of his house. He saw Ryan come out of the Gibbs' house holding a pistol in his hand. Ryan fired at him and the bullet struck him in the right leg. He had to be taken later to hospital.

A Mr O'Callaghan went to No. 60 and, seeing that Mr Gibbs was dead and Mrs Gibbs was seriously wounded, went to phone for an ambulance. Mrs Gibbs was conveyed to St. Margaret's Hospital at Swindon where she later died.

The next fatality happened to be the clerk to the Newbury Magistrates, Mr Ian Francis Playle. He had driven to Hungerford with his wife, who was a nurse, and two children on their way to Swindon in their blue Ford Sierra. They were driving along Priory Road having passed the John O' Gaunt school when Mrs Playle heard the engine of their car whine, the power abate and a crack in the windscreen. As she turned to her husband for an explanation, she saw that he was bleeding profusely from a wound in his neck. Their car travelled across the road as Mrs Playle attempted to turn the engine off, but they struck a Reliant Robin parked at the side. Mrs Playle tried to staunch the flow of blood coming from her husband's injury. A couple of men rushed to where the blue Ford Sierra had come to rest. One of them applied a towel to Mr Playle's neck wound, whilst the other attempted first aid under Mrs Playle's instructions. Despite their ministrations, Mr Playle was to die later from his injury. He was the last person killed by Ryan.

Ryan continued on his way, wounding a Mr George Noon, who happened to be visiting his son's family in Priory Road. Mr Noon, struck in the shoulder and right eye, was the last person injured by Ryan. Ryan was now seen to be running along Priory Road, firing his revolver indiscriminately as he went. He entered the grounds of the John O'Gaunt School and went to the school's changing rooms.

Whilst all this had been happening the Police had not, of course, been inactive. They had been inundated with telephone calls from the public[1], as were other emergency services and Police Officers had set up road blocks around the town, although so confusing was the situation and so hurried the response that people were still able to enter Hungerford. This would happen, of course, under the circumstances prevailing and no amount of Police on the scene of the horrendous incident that was unfolding in the Berkshire town at the time could prevent mistakes occurring, especially in the early stages. The Police had also set up their Incident Room at the Police Station in Park Street.

Thames Valley Police had, shortly after the formation of the force, organised a Support Group which, as its name implies, were able to go anywhere in the force area to supplement the local Police. Within the Group was a very highly trained Tactical Firearms Team under the command of a middle ranking Police Officer. In 1987 that person was Chief Inspector Glyn Lambert. He had to ensure that not only did firearms officers attend the scene as quickly as possible in an effort to 'contain' the situation, but also that dog handlers and other specialist officers were able to be present should they be required.

Also serving with the team in 1987 were two Inspectors, each supervising two squads of eight men with a Sergeant in charge of each squad.

A crucial part of the training of this Unit, as well as other firearms trained Officers in the Thames Valley Police, was not only when to use a gun but also when not to use one. It was often pointed out, quite forcibly on the regular training days that were held throughout the force area, that any fool could use a gun; it needed a sensible person

---

1 There were half a million telephone calls recorded. According to one Police Officer who took an active part in the operation, "It was absolute 'melt down'." Matters were not helped by the fact that the Police were receiving reports of incidents that had occurred some time previously. They were obviously well meant but they added to the confusion.

to use one responsibly. An apt slogan that was displayed on the walls of the various firearm ranges dotted about the Thames Valley Police District was, 'Think it out. Don't shoot it out!'

These training sessions emphasised this time and time again and very high standards were demanded of all the Thames Valley Police firearms trained Officers, not just in accuracy of firing a gun but in the handling and the tactical use of them. Should 'Authorised Firearms Officers' not come up to scratch they were de-authorised very quickly.

One of these highly trained Officers was Sergeant (later Inspector) Paul Brightwell who had joined the Police in 1970 and had served at various towns throughout the Thames Valley Police Area before

Police Sergeant Paul Brightwell.
He attempted to talk Michael Ryan into surrendering himself.

going onto the Traffic Department and then joining the Support Group. He had left 'the Group' when he had been promoted to Sergeant but had rejoined in early 1987 to head one of the teams comprising the Unit.

On the morning of Wednesday, 19th August he had been on a training session on the Army range at Otmoor near the Police Headquarters at Kidlington, when his and other Police Officers' pagers went off as the appalling situation at Hungerford became apparent.

At first it was a 'shooting incident' that the Unit's Officers were attending, something that they had done so often before. As they set off on the long journey through the Oxfordshire and Berkshire countryside to reach Hungerford, naturally apprehensive as to what they were approaching, it was only as they listened to the 'traffic' on their car radios that the scale of the terrible tragedy that was unfolding in the town became known to them.

In the meantime, P.C. Brereton's colleague P.C. Wood was operating as the Command vehicle whilst Thames Valley Police mounted their response to the shocking circumstances. He had kept Police Headquarters informed as to what was going on, clearing the vicinity of people and setting up a roadblock, whilst requesting the use of Police marksmen.

Whilst some firearms trained Officers did arrive they were from the Protection team, trained in close quarter protection rather than pursuit and containment of offenders.

When the men of the Firearms Teams did arrive they were hurriedly briefed within the confines of the small, antiquated Police Station. They also heard the name of Michael Ryan for the first time.

Sergeant Brightwell and his men left the Police Station with copies of the town map hurriedly thrust into their hands and cautiously made their way towards the school, which they believed their quarry had entered. As the teams warily approached the school, they were not

116

helped by the fact that curtains at the open windows of houses were flapping in the breeze and they had to pause and consider whether it was Ryan peeking out through the windows or just the curtains blowing naturally. Each, of course, had to be checked thoroughly. As the Police apprehensively edged their way towards the school, they noticed Mr Barnard's car with bullet holes running up the bonnet to where he had been struck.

Another problem the Police encountered were the press helicopters hovering over Hungerford, the noise effectively blocking out their personal radios, making it extremely difficult to maintain contact with one another. Members of the public, seeing the Police as they advanced, came out with cups of tea. "Just like when the Army first went into Northern Ireland," recalls one Officer.[2] Eventually they reached the school and Sergeant Brightwell and P.C. 2606 Anthony Bates had a clear view of the buildings. The Tactical teams had achieved one of their aims. 'Identify, locate and contain!' Now they had to keep in mind another, which was uppermost in their minds, 'Safety of the public, safety of the Police, safety of the subject.'

As they watched, P.C. Bates noticed the Kalashnikov rifle with a white flag attached to the barrel being thrown through a window of the school.

Sergeant Brightwell settled down and began the lengthy process of negotiation with Ryan in an effort to ultimately draw the man out and into Police custody, without any danger to either the Police engaged in the siege, members of the public or even to Ryan himself.

For over an hour the patient Police Sergeant spoke to Ryan, urging him to surrender, parrying his questions about what had taken place that grim afternoon; trying all the time to coax him out of his place of containment. At one point, Sergeant David Warwick, a senior firearm instructor in the Thames Valley Police held Ryan within the sight of his rifle. Bearing in mind that at this particular stage in the proceedings Ryan was posing no direct threat to either his colleagues or members of the public, Sergeant Warwick did not fire the round

2 *Comment by Inspector Brightwell.*

117

that would have stopped the siege there and then. All the training that he had received over the years and which he himself had imparted to other members of the Police Service steeled the Sergeant in his determination not to casually shoot Ryan, although he was a known and dangerous murderer, whilst that man was not actually endangering any other person.

The two Sergeants, in their own way and independent of each other, determined that, if possible, the matter would be resolved peacefully and that Ryan, no matter that he was a mass murderer, would be taken into custody and delivered up to someone else in higher authority to judge the issues involved that day.

Sergeant Brightwell persevered in his attempt to persuade Ryan to come out of the school. At 6.52pm he heard a shot from the room occupied by him. The Sergeant called out to him several times but there was no response.

A Police helicopter was called up to scan the building but nothing could be seen. A Police team entered the school and searched one floor at a time. Reaching the roof, one Officer, P.C. Robertson, looked over the roof with a mirror and saw the lifeless body of Ryan. Even then the Police could not relax their vigilance. Carefully entering the room where Ryan lay, they had to place a rope around his body, leave the room and pull the rope in case it was booby-trapped.

Sergeant Warwick observed that in Ryan's right hand was a 9mm. Beretta pistol. Upon closer inspection he could see that Ryan had a bullet wound on the right-hand side of his temple and an exit wound on his left-hand side.

The siege of Hungerford was over; the agony, however, was to go on.

Whenever a murder is committed it follows that a thorough investigation by the Police has to be conducted. Where the suspect is alive and has been taken into custody, the Senior Investigating Officer has to submit a full report to the Director of Public

Prosecutions for the case to be prosecuted eventually at Crown Court. When the suspect is dead, a full report still has to be prepared for the attention of the Chief Constable of the force area. Any sudden or unnatural deaths have also to be reported to the local Coroner for a full Inquest to be held at a later date. It may be that, unless a public enquiry is held, the Coroner's Inquest will be the only Court to hear the full circumstances of the deaths.

So it was in this case, and, because of the horrific nature of the crimes, the numbers involved, the suicide of the suspect and the complexity, Detective Superintendent John Childerley was appointed to be in overall charge of the investigation.

A Major Investigation Incident Room was set up. Usually it is as close to the scene as possible and a good place would be the local Police Station. However, because it was going to prove a vast undertaking and Hungerford Police Station is comparatively small, it was decided that it should be situated at the Thames Valley Police Training Centre at Sulhampstead, several miles away along the Bath Road. Teams of Police Officers were sent out to interview witnesses and obtain long and detailed statements from them which would then be collated at Sulhampstead and submitted with the necessary report to the Assistant Chief Constable (Operations) at Police Headquarters, Kidlington.

In the meantime, the funeral of P.C. Brereton took place at the parish church of Shaw-cum-Donnington with family, friends and a large contingent of Police Officers from Thames Valley and other forces in attendance. A Guard of Honour provided by the Police lined the path leading to the entrance to the church, whilst P.C. Brereton's coffin was carried by six Policemen into the church, covered by the flag of the Thames Valley Police. Also in the congregation were the Chief Constable of Thames Valley, Colin Smith (now Her Majesty's Inspector of Constabulary), Peter Imbert, the Commissioner of the Metropolitan Police and formerly Chief Constable of Thames Valley (now Lord Imbert), and the Home Secretary, Douglas Hurd (now Lord Hurd). Colin Smith, in paying his respects to the fallen officer said, "His cheerful disposition and irrepressible sense of humour gained him many friends both within the service and the community, as is evidenced here today." Mr. Smith mentioned the work that P.C. Brereton had done on behalf of the Royal Ulster Constabulary's Widows and Orphans and, speaking directly to his widow, continued, " Liz, I was in Northern Ireland last Friday and the R.U.C. asked me to convey their condolences to you. No group of men and women in this country can better appreciate your feelings, which makes their good wishes the greater valued." Mr Smith then went on, " It is so tragic but perhaps appropriate if his life had to be so cruelly cut short that he should die when aware of the risk. He went right in to the very centre of a very dangerous situation with the clear intention of trying to save the lives of the people of Hungerford and to uphold the Queen's Peace."

The funerals for the other victims took place all through that dreadful month.

In September, the Inquest into those killed in Hungerford was held. (As Mrs Godfrey was murdered in Wiltshire, her Inquest was conducted at Swindon.) After listening to the witnesses, the Coroner, Charles Hoile, in his summing up to the jury, commented, "... There is an inherent conflict between the desire to retain an unarmed Police Force on the one hand and the easy and early availability of arms on the other. So far as the Police response is concerned, leaving aside the armed branch of the Force or that part of the Force which can become armed, the response of the Police obviously was pretty prompt because quite early one of the first people to be killed was P.C. Brereton answering the call and he was not alone. He was with another officer in another vehicle and two other officers who were local Policemen called to the emergency. Looking at it from that view their response would be difficult to fault..." After listening to all the witnesses the jury came to the only conclusion they could possibly reach, that of 'Unlawful killing.'[3] They added their commendation to P.C.s Brereton, Wood, Maggs and Sergeant Ryan for their actions that day. They did make one recommendation however through their foreman.[4] "The Jury do feel that semi-automatic weapons should not generally be available and that an individual should not be allowed to own an unlimited quantity of arms and ammunition. However, knowing that the subject is under review by the Government, the Jury make no detailed recommendations." (This was a reference to the Firearms Act that allowed people to buy and acquire arms and ammunition on a wholesale basis and which was later amended.)

There was a flurry of criticism of the Police actions at Hungerford, "Why had they done this? Why hadn't they done that?" and an enquiry was carried out by Her Majesty's Inspector of Constabulary. In due course he issued his report. He stated that having examined the events at Hungerford and having reviewed the American experience, it was his considered opinion that the general arming of the Police would not prevent a similar incident occurring again.

He commented on the communications problem experienced by Thames Valley Police and made certain recommendations as to the availability and control of VHF channels and the use of portable VHF radios. He also made further recommendations in respect of communications and the more widespread use of helicopters at such incidents and also that the use of armoured vehicles at such incidents should be considered. Her Majesty's Inspector noted that it had not helped that on 19th August 1987, Hungerford Police Station was undergoing refurbishment and it was further recommended that alternative arrangements would be needed to deal with a major incident if or when it occurred.

---

3 A similar verdict was given at Mrs Godfrey's Inquest.   4 Sergeant Peter Ryan and Constable Bernard Maggs both received Chief Constables Commendations for the brave manner in which they carried out their duties, and the following; Superintendent Joseph Fox, Inspector Colin Gibbens, Sergeant Daniel Sullivan, Sergeant George Wilson and Constables Walter Skerrett, Roger Cooper, Christopher Larkin and Lawrence Workman for their professionalism and dedication to duty.

In June 1988 it was announced officially that several participants in what was to become known as the 'Hungerford Massacre' had been awarded the Queen's Commendation for Brave Conduct for their actions on 19th August 1987.

They were; Linda Bright and Hazel Haslett, Ambulancewomen; Carol Hall, Air Stewardess; Carl Peter Lawrence Harries, Lance Corporal, Royal Engineers; Michael Thomas Palmer, Supervisor, Newbury District Council; David John Sparrow, Lifeguard and attendant, Newbury District Council; Police Constable Roger Brereton and Police Constable Jeremy John Wood.

H.R.H. Prince Charles later presented these awards to the recipients. Mrs Elizabeth Brereton of course received the award on behalf of her late husband.

POLICE OFFICERS
WITHIN THE THAMES VALLEY POLICE DISTRICT
KILLED BY CRIMINAL ACTION

POLICE CONSTABLE JOSEPH HILARY GILKES:

JOINED METROPOLITAN POLICE...1868
RESIGNED...1868
JOINED OXFORD CITY POLICE..1869
DIED ON DUTY..1869

INSPECTOR JOSEPH DREWITT:

JOINED BERKSHIRE CONSTABULARY.......................................1859
PROMOTED SERGEANT...1872
PROMOTED INSPECTOR..1876
MURDERED ON DUTY...1876

POLICE CONSTABLE THOMAS SHORTER:

JOINED BERKSHIRE CONSTABULARY.......................................1874
MURDERED ON DUTY...1876

POLICE CONSTABLE JOHN JOSEPH CHARLTON:

JOINED BERKSHIRE CONSTABULARY.......................................1882
RESIGNED...1882
REJOINED BERKSHIRE CONSTABULARY...................................1886
KILLED ON DUTY..1899

INSPECTOR FRANCIS JOHN EAST:

JOINED BERKSHIRE CONSTABULARY.......................................1923
PROMOTED SERGEANT...1935
PROMOTED INSPECTOR..1943
DIED OF INJURIES RECEIVED ON DUTY...................................1944

INSPECTOR JAMES BRADLEY:
JOINED OXFORDSHIRE CONSTABULARY.......................................1946
PROMOTED SERGEANT...1962
PROMOTED INSPECTOR...1966
DIED OF INJURIES RECEIVED ON DUTY...1967

DETECTIVE CONSTABLE IAN COWARD:
JOINED BERKSHIRE CONSTABULARY...1961
DIED OF INJURIES RECEIVED ON DUTY...1971

POLICE CONSTABLE ROGER BRERETON:
JOINED THAMES VALLEY POLICE...1973
MURDERED ON DUTY...1987

INDEX

127

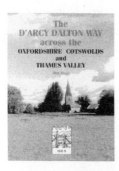

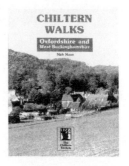

The D'Arcy Dalton Way:
Across the Oxfordshire Cotswolds
and Thames Valley.

Chiltern Walks:
Oxon and West Bucks.

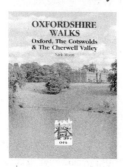

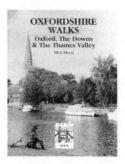

Oxfordshire Walks Volume 1:
Oxfords, the Cotswolds and the
Cherwell Valley.

Oxfordshire Walks Volume 2:
Oxford, the Downs and the
Thames Valley.

A selection of books by Nick Moon, covering Oxfordshire and surrounding area, eachcontaining circular walks. These books are written in association with The Oxford Fieldpaths Society.

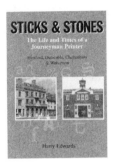

STICKS & STONES
The Life and Times of a Journeyman Printer
Hertford, Dunstable, Cheltenham & Wolverton
by **Harry Edwards**

Sticks and Stones recounts the story of the author's journey through his life in the printing industry, from printer's devil until retirement. Leaving school at the age of fourteen, Harry's transition from schoolboy to apprentice was abrupt. The printing world, with its own language, customs and tradition, was strange at first but most of the journeymen were kind and helpful to a young lad, covering up for many a mistake in the first formative years. The journey begins in Hertfordshire, then takes him on to Bedfordshire, Gloucestershire, London and finally to Buckinghamshire. It follows the author's progress as he seeks not only promotion but also the opportunity to become involved in the latest technology, be it cold type composition, photocomposition, or computer aided typesetting. He touches briefly on his private life when it is appropriate, but the story is primarily about how the changes in the printing industry affected him. The author is now retired and lives in Milton Keynes.

SANCTITY & SCANDAL
in Bedfordshire & Buckinghamshire
by John Houghton

Some of the holy places in this book were monasteries, priories and churches. Some of the people were priests and preachers. Some were saints and some were sinners. And as for the unholy times, they included wars and civil unrest, religious upheaval, and not a little scandal. So in the two neighbouring counties of Beds and Bucks are true tales of persecution and plunder, of faithful pastors, and misbehaving ministers. Read about the bent solicitor, he triggered off litigation which went on for 205 years! It robbed St.Paul's Church of the endowments of the Hospital of St.John in Bedford. In Bucks there is the astonishing behaviour of the twice-obsessed Vicar of water Stratford who was responsible for extraordinary scenes of corporate mania in 1694. There was John Wesley who could ride 90 miles in a day. On horseback he rode 4000 miles a year-altogether in his lifetime 250,000 miles. He preached 40,000 sermons, many of them in Bedford which he visited 32 times. But Bedford had its own homegrown evangelist too, Timothy Matthews, who blew his own trumpet, but only to collect a crowd to hear his preaching. The pen also has its place too as well as the preaching - Bunyan of Bedford, and Milton in Bucks. Not forgetting William Cole, Bletchley's clerical diarist. Keach, the Baptist pastor of Winslow was twice put in the stocks but that didn't stop him preaching even while he was exposed to public ridicule. Here in this book is just a sample collection of holy places and people set in unholy times in Beds and Bucks.

All royalties from this book will be donated to Willen Hospice and St. Martin's Church, Fenny Stratford.

CHANGES IN OUR LANDSCAPE:
Aspects of Bedfordshire, Buckinghamshire
and the Chilterns 1947-1992
by Eric Meadows

In the post-War years, this once quiet rural backwater between Oxford and Cambridge has undergone growth and change - and the expert camera of Eric Meadows has captured it all.... An enormous variety of landscape, natural and man-made, from yesteryear and today - open downs and rolling farmland, woods and commons, ancient earthworks, lakes and moats, vanished elms Quarries, nature reserves and landscape gardens. Many building styles- churches of all periods, stately homes and town dwellings, rural pubs, gatehouses and bridges. Secluded villages contrast their timeless lifestyle with the bustle of modern developing towns and their industries. Distilled from a huge collection of 25,000 photographs, this book offers the author's personal selection of over 350 that best display the area's most attractive features and its notable changes over 50 years. The author's detailed captions and notes complete a valuable local history. The original hardback edition was in print for only 4 weeks in 1992. By popular demand now in a large format paperback.

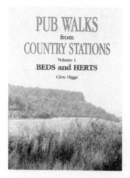
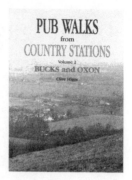

PUB WALKS FROM COUNTRY STATIONS:
Volume 1 Beds and Herts

&

PUB WALKS FROM COUNTRY STATIONS:
Volume 2 Bucks and Oxon
by Clive Higgs

Two titles both containing fourteen circular country rambles, each starting and finishing at a railway station and incorporating a pub-stop at a mid-way point.

Volume 1 has 5 walks in Bedfordshire starting from Sandy, Biggleswade, Harlington, Flitwick and Linslade. Together with 9 walks in Hertfordshire starting from Watford, Kings Langley, Boxmoor, Berkhamsted, Tring, Stanstead St.Margaret's, Watton-at Stone, Bricket Wood and Harpenden.

Volume 2 has 9 walks in Buckingham starting from Gerrards Cross, Beaconsfield, Saunderton, Princes Risborough, Amersham, Chesham, Great Missenden, Stoke Manderville and Wendover. Together with 5 walks in Oxfordshire starting from Goring-on-Thames, Cholsey, Lower Shiplake, Islip and Hanborough Station.

The shortest walk is a distance of 4miles and the longest 7 and a half miles.

BUCKINGHAMSHIRE MURDERS
by Len Woodley

Thoroughly researched accounts of seventeen murders ranging across the old County of Buckinghamshire. Commencing from the early nineteenth century right up to modern times. You will read about the Newton Longville shop-keeper murdered for a few shillings; the Dagnall killer; murders for no apparent reason at Buckingham and Denham; the unsolved murder of the canal man at Slough; love affairs that went tragically wrong at Burnham and Bourne End; a fatal ambush at Botolph Claydon; the Pole who wanted to be shot and a fellow country-man who escaped justice by fleeing to the Soviet Union. There is the trooper who slew his girlfriend at Slough and hid the body under the mattress; the W.R.A.F girl who offered to baby-sit but met a killer instead; the bright young girl who went for a last walk down a country lane and the couple who were the victims of a man's obsession with himself!

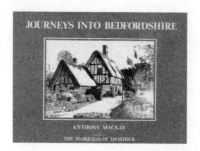

JOURNEYS INTO BEDFORDSHIRE
&
JOURNEYS INTO BUCKINGHAMSHIRE
by Anthony Mackay

These two books of ink drawings reveal an intriguing historic heritage and capture the spirit of England's rural heartland, ranging widely over cottages and stately homes, over bridges, churches and mills, over sandy woods, chalk downs and watery river valleys. Every corner of Bedfordshire and Buckinghamshire has been explored in the search for material, and, although the choice of subjects is essentially a personal one, the resulting collection represents a unique record of the environment today. The notes and maps, which accompany the drawings, lend depth to the books, and will assist others on their own journeys around the counties. Anthony Mackay's pen-and-ink drawings are of outstanding quality. An architectural graduate, he is equally at home depicting landscapes and buildings. The medium he uses is better able to show both depth and detail than any photograph.